T0381230

MILLION DOLLAR AGENT

New Generation of Real Estate

TAV SCHEMBRI

Contents

Preface v

Chapter 1   Introduction - How it all started 1

Chapter 2   Market Your Best Self 5

Chapter 3   Dreaded Cold Calls – New Clients.............................18

Chapter 4   Be Positive...29

Chapter 5   Your Mindset is Your Success 41

Chapter 6   Mindset in Business...49

Chapter 7   Develop and Manage Your Client's Trust...................53

Chapter 8   Provide Worth...63

Chapter 9   Be Successful with Your Best Dressed Self...............67

Chapter 10 How Does Your Vehicle Present? 75

Chapter 11 Stay in Touch 80

Chapter 12 Work-Life Balance 89

Chapter 13 Be Authentic 97

Chapter 14 Be The Best You Can Be.. 110

Chapter 15 Final Word of Guidance 125

Preface

This book has come about as a result of many exchanges that have come across my path with various levels of real-estate professionals and a great amount of youth that have had an interest in Real Estate. There has been much conversation and ensuing questions relating to how I have been able to successfully master my craft in Real Estate. It was simply time for me to share this with my fellow colleagues and general public so that everyone that was interested in this powerful book could benefit. The goal for me was to give the reader a hand-up in the industry that has been so good to me.

Being a Top Producer for Remax and achieving as high as 18th Worldwide in the Industry within the first year of becoming an Agent, has made me realize that if I was able to accomplish this feat, then the majority of people would also be able to do this. However, I noticed agents becoming their own worst enemy and it was clear to me that they were fighting a losing battle. From my first day to present, having been in the business for just six short, yet jam-packed years, is the reason that I have people interested in this book announcement. I was adamant in not reinventing the wheel as some educators string you along to get them to buy into their system. I know people will find the information useful for advancing themselves and CATAPULTING themselves into the upper echelon of the industry instantly. You will find that the content on the following pages are so important to everyone's success.

CHAPTER 1

Introduction - How it all started

My parents immigrated to Canada, from Sicily in 1958, a year before I was born in 1959. Their hopes, just as many people who immigrated here, were that Canada would offer our family exciting future life opportunities. When they first arrived, they landed in Regent Park, in the heart of Toronto. We were a first-generation Italian family, growing up on the south side of Regent Park surrounded by projects, in a rather tough part of the city.

My siblings and I learned the value of hard work from our parents. Because of my environment, I was forced to be street smart at a very young age and to grow up fast. Having blue-collar parents, I was not encouraged academically because in those days, putting food on the table was the number one priority. It wasn't long after I was born, that my parents bought their first property in East York.

To help fund my teen years, I took summer jobs working in the construction industry which I'm sure, is where the original seed was planted in me for real estate, and developed my fascination for buildings and properties in all their intricacies. It wasn't until after high school that I moved into the Brampton, Ontario area. Once in Brampton, I met the love of my life, Maria. We met at a mutual friend's wedding in Montreal. It wasn't long before she moved to Toronto and we began our marriage journey together. She is still my pillar. I could not do without her continuous support.

My first passion and experience as a businessman was in the hairdressing industry, in which I met many people with their varied personalities and all of this taught me how important and valuable this life and communication skills are to each of us. During this period, I formed some exceptional friendships. During my time as a stylist, I eventually opened a total of 5 hairdressing salons throughout Toronto and GTA. I have been asked on numerous occasions how I ended up doing hair for a living and my response is always, it was just fun for me. I am very good at the relationship aspect of life and this was a great catalyst to do what I loved and have fun doing it. There were some incredible people that came into my salons over the years. I'm grateful for meeting every one of them.

One of my favourite pastimes is wood-working. It keeps me grounded and centered and I find great peace in getting lost in this craft. Part of a well-balanced life in my opinion are hobbies. We need to do something that exists outside of work in our leisure time; an activity that brings us joy and takes us away from our usual day-to-day routine for a peaceful release. I still believe this is the way to enjoy a balanced life.

However, unfortunately, or some may say, fortunately, an accident happened that changed the trajectory of my life. Literally, in one moment in time, I lost two of my fingers because of the woodworking accident. The hobby I love rendered me with eight fingers; as you could imagine, losing an index finger and a middle finger created an obstacle in hairdressing. However, after the surgery and a few months of healing, I went back to hairdressing for a few years.

Although this accident that happened to me, I must share with you that I really didn't find it life-altering. In fact, it wasn't until the nurses and specialists at the hospital mentioned that I might need some counselling because of the incident that I started questioning my feelings regarding the accident and wondering if I should have felt different about it. So I decided the best thing for me to do was to leave the hospital. I felt the experience was negative seed planting that I didn't want to be part of.

The change in trajectory that I mentioned earlier came about several years ago when Maria and I sold one of our properties. This re-kindled my appetite for real estate, bringing the love of buying and selling back up to the surface. Thus, with some serious deliberation, we decided the next chapter in our life would in fact be real estate. And that's precisely what happened in 2013, my wife and I opened our Satellite Office in Caledon Ontario. And my Journey began!

I proudly wore the title of #1 Real Estate Agent in Caledon Ontario, for the three years in total, 2016-2018, in Volume Sales. Additionally, I have sat in the top 100 agents Worldwide and Canada year over year under the RE/MAX banner.

This feat brings me to this point in my life and my desire to help you— the novice Real Estate Professional in your journey in trying to make a living doing what you will come to love. This lifestyle doesn't come easily; I have worked very hard to get where I am and have been fortunate in the past six years since we started on this Journey.

I want to give back to this industry by sharing this book with you, *Million Dollar Agent; "The New Generation of Real Estate Professionals."* You will find simple, sound advice to catapult you to success.

CHAPTER 2

Market Your Best Self

You've completed your studies and now you're officially licensed. That is thrilling and congratulations to you! This can be both exciting and scary at the same time, because now things are going to get real. And now it's time to start earning a living in the industry you've just studied for and have learned to love throughout the process. You may be thinking, I've got this and I'm ready to get out there and start making millions of dollars. You might be thinking I'm ready and I'm chomping at the bit to get on with my career. Alternatively, you may be on the sidelines wondering what you've gotten yourself into. Either way, this book will help all of you. Rather than re-inventing the wheel, I want to share some of my successful practices to help you build a strong career right off the top!

Let me tell you about my first few deals, which by the way were cultivated from talking to some of my former hairdressing clients. The first was a local farmer, close to the area where I set up my office. I called him because we had an existing relationship. And as it turned out, he was looking to sell his rather large farm and because he knew me and trusted me, we were able to work together. Rule number one, don't let your relationships fade away or worse, die. We ended up doing business together because of this relationship and because we have what I often refer to as conversations. I keep in touch with this man and still have warm respects for him as he helped me lay the foundation to move up and onward in Real Estate.

My second client was also a former hairdressing client. This was another instance of not letting an existing relationship fade away. I reached out to him and many others that were clients and the timing was perfect for me. He knew me and he trusted me and as a result, he was only too happy to work with me. Not every story in Real estate is this cut and dry and I did spend an awful lot of time with him. In total, he and I viewed some 45 homes before he found the one he wanted. Therefore, not everything comes in a tiny and perfect little package, especially in this industry. Always expect the unexpected.

As a licenced Agent, it was time for me to start marketing myself and doing the work — I had to start somewhere and the logical place to start was with my Sphere of Influence and contacts such as school friends and business clients. This was easy for me and it was how I built the foundation for my successful business. Sometimes in life, it's just good timing, plain and simple. Most of the time though, it's determination and hard work. But marketing always includes conversations whether you are cold calling or reaching out to existing contacts, friends or family members. Keep this in mind though, whether you talk about kids, jobs, sports, weather, business or anything in between, there is always something you can find to talk about; which is a healthy gateway for any business person regardless of whether you're seasoned or novice.

Discussions are key to marketing yourself in this industry; I cannot highlight this strongly enough. It is the key for success and it's how I have done and continue to conduct myself in all junctions of business. And I'll tell you something — people love to talk, they love to talk about themselves and people love to talk about real estate with a professional in the industry. Everybody wants to know how much their house is worth, they want to know the market conditions, and they want to know the best time to sell should they consider doing so. Even if they are not in the market to sell, people are just naturally curious about real estate conditions in general because it's such an enormous part of our economy.

Where marketing is concerned, I have to say don't be afraid of the traditional practice of making cold calls and door knocking. These are tools in your marketing toolbox that will always be less than savoury to do, but will likely have the most impact and increase on your chances of success in sales. The thing is that you never know who is considering a move.

Marketing through advertising and signage is also key to compliment the conversation aspect, you want to be seen and be branded. Do your best to find a niche branding that you like and that works for you and the important thing here is to stick to it. The more you waiver and change things up, the less dependable and noticeable you are and less top of mind. Right now, you are at an important time in the sales cycle — in the beginning.

When you get into a slump (and you will at some point) and you're tired of making the same old prospecting calls, you might want to try these below ideas when it's time to find fresh prospects and re-activate your sales funnel. There are always ways to be creative in this market and take chances and get out there. And ask yourself this question, what have you got to lose?

- **Emailing** is a helpful tool to uncover hidden opportunities. Email is a great way to connect with people as this is accessible worldwide and your recipient can review it at their own leisure. Ask open-ended questions and try to prompt the recipient to reply. You might be surprised at how your next opportunity can be found.

- How about good old-fashioned **snail mail**. You know the kind of mail that needs a postage stamp. These days, everyone is so swamped with online mail, yourself included, that it is nice to get the occasional piece of real mail carried right to your door, and it can even have ink on paper, just like the old days!

- **Token Appreciations**: Another possibility for you to consider is you can try Thank You cards with Starbuck's or Tim Horton gift certificates, anniversary and birthday cards. Small little inexpensive tokens, people really appreciate these items because they know you are thinking about them. And of course, you want to be sure to include your business card.

- **Social Media:** Make it light and fun! The idea is to get people to start sharing your post. Ask your friends to share it. Most people want to help you, it is human nature, so you may find that people are agreeable to sharing your posts. If you can make your post a little edgy and fun, all the better. Set Yourself Up For Social. Make sure you have social media accounts on all the big networks — Facebook, Twitter, Pinterest, LinkedIn, and even Instagram if you snap a lot of house pics. Interact with users, share good press, and promote, promote and promote your properties.

Add **social** sharing to property pages. Chances are, home shoppers are eager to share their top housing pics with friends and family, so make it easy for home buyers to email and share various properties online by adding social sharing buttons. Never miss an opportunity to have someone market your listing.

Website: Make your website mobile-friendly. Today's consumers spend tons of time on their mobile devices. In fact, a recent study has shown that 51.7% of internet searches in 2018 use their mobile devices for online activity. It is paramount that your website is mobile-friendly.

While real estate agents are still key in the home-buying process, buyers are increasingly looking to do more leg work online before involving an expert. A study from the National Association of Realtors showed that 92% of buyers use the internet to begin house hunting, driving home the need for real estate agents to have a vigorous online presence. If you are not active, engaging, and networking online, then you are missing out.

- If you are not out there and interacting and **networking**, it's unreasonable to expect to meet new people. Keep in mind some simple ways to meet new people, join a local gym, community centre, or running group, whatever speaks to you. Or better yet, offer to speak at a function in your local community. Become an expert, and again, make it fun because people will talk about your speaking and you want it to be memorable. And through this, you'll become the go-to person in real estate in your niche. At the very least, you will certainly make some new friends, and find a new buyer or seller in the course.

Make yourself easy to contact. Put your contact info on every page of your website. Ideally, make an impressive "contact us" page that grabs attention. Try to think outside the box and do things different than the masses. And answer your phone!

Create a great business card. Get an awesome-looking business card and hand them out at every single opportunity that you come across.

- Existing clients or prospects can be valuable to **stay connected** with. If you have done your homework, you will have information on them and you can use this to your advantage. As an example, you can call an existing prospect up that you know has a very well-kept property. And ask, "Who does your lawn?" Why? You need the referral for another client. First of all, it is flattering to have someone compliment your property. Second, it is an opportunity to open an otherwise closed or slightly ajar door.

- **CRM** (customer relationship management software): This software allows you to put any and all information about existing and prospective clients into one tidy program. This will help you tremendously in business. You may have noticed already that low performers are often complaining or they have many excuses for the lack of leads. The truth of the matter is that there are sufficient leads, however, you must do the work. What tends to happen is that we make our hot leads or current clients the priority and neglect the warm or cooler leads. Reasonable, right? The advice I want to give here is, *always have multiple funnels* — hot, warm and cold. Keep all of them top of mind.

- Everyone loves **referrals** from other real estate agents. But for many agents, getting a referral from an out-of-area agent is more a matter of coincidence than the result of any concentrated effort. It doesn't have to be that way. We have agents in our industry who have mastered agent-to-agent referrals as a fully sustainable method of producing business. The key is being deliberate about it, not simply waiting for a lead to happen.

As well as the major points noted above, here are some additional real estate marketing ideas to help you succeed in the industry.

- **Keep an eye on your competition**. What are other realtors in your area doing? What do their websites look like? How active are they on social media? Take note of what competitors are doing, then avoid their mistakes and replicate their success.

- **Use local images**. You are not just selling a house, you are selling your area of expertise. Highlight the best that your area has to offer, with high-quality photos of local town or city landmarks and familiar sites. Hire a photo professional. Successful real estate relies heavily on great images. Bad photos will weaken interest in even the most amazing properties. It is essential that you have beautiful photos of your properties. Hire a professional whenever possible. Just remember this is one of those scenarios when it pays to bring in the professionals.

- **Create a virtual tour**. Your clients' time is precious, and they want to understand as much as possible about a property prior to visiting in person. Virtual tours are a fantastic way to give a complete, accurate preview of the property for potential buyers. And if done right, this will lure serious potential clients to your property.

- **Local sponsorship**. This is something I do as a customary practice. You can consider helping sponsor local festivals, sports teams, or school events. Signing up as a local sponsor often means getting your business a spot-on T-shirt, program pamphlets, or flyers.

Have a newsletter. Email marketing is one of the best strategies for building client relationships. Collect emails from your website, local outreach, or any other methods you can think of. Send your email subscribers the stuff they are looking for, such as notices about upcoming open houses, new houses on the market, news about seminars you are offering in the area, etc.

Google my business page. Google My Business is the latest in Google location-based pages. If you are feeling confused, do not worry, it is the same idea as Google Places for Businesses. Setting up a Google My Business account makes it easy for users to find you in Google Search and Google Maps. Trust me, this one is a no-brainer.

Learn your niche. If you've got some real estate marketing competition in your area, you may want to consider making yourself stand out by going niche. Become the go-to real estate agent for dog owners, families with kids, divorced persons, farm land owners or whatever. Making a name for yourself around a specific niche can make you memorable.

Paid social ads. Do not be afraid to take some paid ads on social media. With organic reach dwindling on many popular social networks like Facebook, paid Facebook ads are often the most effective way to get in front of clients. Facebook has tons of great targeting features that ensure you are only paying to get noticed by your key target audiences.

- ***Get an advertorial*** for each season into local magazines. When it comes to real estate, it is important that you get hyper-focused on local. Getting yourself in local magazines or newspapers is a wonderful way to get the word out about you and your brand. Write a column or feature advertorial for local publications. Highlight your knowledge, or your volunteer efforts or philanthropy, plus local market conditions everyone wants to know, rising prices, interest rates future development, etc. or list the reasons why your regional area is becoming more popular. Make yourself a knowledgeable member of your community. Remember, marketing today is all about inbound, and that does not just apply online. Users want you to share some of your knowledge for free before investing time and money in you.

- ***Brand, brand & brand.*** As you may have gathered, branding matters! And it is easy and relatively inexpensive to do things to enhance your branding efforts like buy pens, cups, coasters or whatever in bulk. Give out branded goodies at local festivals and events to spread your brand. Just keep handing these goodies out just like you would your business cards.

Because this is such an imperative topic, it might be the single biggest thing you get right that will positively affect your business growth. And let's face it, you can never get enough information and advice on marketing yourself, hence your business. There are some universal areas in which 90% of us quite literally dread, which is where I will start in this next section in Marketing Yourself in Real Estate.

Cold Calling Dread: if you are avoiding cold calling, this can and will negatively impact your ability to turn prospects into clients. Improve your <u>phone prospecting skills</u> and develop a formula or a script that gives you the best bang for your buck.

If you are in a slump and lacking inspiration, it is time to refresh and reconsider your strategies and energize yourself. How do you want to stand out from the crowd?

A good technique is to target expired listings of other agents. By asking smart questions and if there are clear insights, you invite potential sellers to work with you to market their properties in a way that better bring into line, their needs.

Do not misjudge the power of in-person connections. Try these strategies for real estate, and build trust while gaining referrals and inevitably growing your business.

Remain "visible" by subtly adding value to homeowners beyond the one-time sale. Drop off notes in their mail boxes, send a greeting email to let them know you are thinking about them.

Word of mouth" marketing is an immensely powerful tool. Testimonials from satisfied customers are irreplaceable to use in your promotion, both online and in print.

Technology designed for the real estate industry has made the job seem deceivingly easy, so it is important to market your worth. Promote the indispensable value of your skills and expertise on your website.

- Avoid some common newcomer mistakes by rephrasing your discussions with clients in a way that emphasizes your ability and sincere engagement. In psychology, it's taught that if you paraphrase someone, especially in this industry and when you are trying to land a client, it's the best way to let them know that you are listening and that you hear what they want; it's a great tool to practice in business but you will find it is a great tool in life too.

Keep your branding consistent and keep the conversations going. Below are some tips for long-term success in real estate.

This includes and is an especially important aspect of business, especially this one. Let's not fall into the cycle of "insanity" — doing the same thing over and over and expecting different results. This should give you some innovative ideas on how to make a long-term strategy successful.

Your pipeline*: U*nquestionably, the most important part of your long-term strategy, is your sales pipeline. The day of abundance of buyers is gone. In this incredibly unique industry of real estate, you must keep track of people for months and sometimes years before they buy. And let's face it, it is a long-term endeavour to get in the door with some people.

To effectively deal with this is a solid follow-up plan. Relying on sticky notes or notes stuck on a pin on your desk, well, what can I say, how is that working for you? If you don't have a valid CRM software, you can use your calendar, or better yet shared calendar. This keeps you and your team aware of your schedule. You can put follow-up phone calls in the calendar, up to years in advance. And you can get notifications to ring through on your computer or your phone, it's effective for the real estate agent on a budget.

Another way to set up your pipeline is to start having seminars and educational meetings. These are usually attended by people thinking about buying or selling somewhere between three months to two years from the time of the event. While it's not always a source of immediate business, it's a wonderful way to get your long-term plan on the right course and give yourself a sense of security about tomorrow's income.

"Keep Your Sales Pipeline Full By Prospecting Continuously. Always Have More People To See Than You Have Time To See Them." – Brian Tracy

Use assistants. Although you may be thinking this can be a costly endeavour and perhaps it's not in the budget, it's a practical way to manage your business, phone call, referrals and scheduling. This may not seem like the best time to hire an assistant, but if you get your follow-up systems in place and make use of them, then you should have regular business coming in within a short period of time.

And if you're good at asking for and getting referrals, then you'll soon be too busy to follow up reliably on your own without an assistant.

If you have an assistant, you'll have someone to help when you get too busy to keep up with marketing and your new follow-up processes; which in turn will allow you to generate even more business, allowing you to pay for the assistant, and continuing to make more of that million dollars. You can go for a virtual assistant, which will fill in the space of working alone and later, hire a full-time, in-person assistant. Or, you can jump to the end and get a full-time assistant. As a good rule of thumb, before you do that, make sure you have four months' worth of salary and tax money saved. Even if they're good, it will take about this long before you see a return on your investment.

Be self-sufficient. Real estate professionals don't think about what will happen to their business if their broker closes or sells. This is where it's important to become self-sufficient. Business needs to come from your own efforts rather than that of the office you work with and for. This will ensure that if something goes sideways in the brokerage that you are working under, you will still have your business. You might be a go-getter when you go to another broker and could result in lower fees if you come with a good business base.

You need to get and foster relationships. Real estate specialists have their areas of ability, but buyers don't. This is just smart business. I have many contacts with real estate agents throughout Toronto and the GTA and I find referrals that arise from these relationship building.

Your client recommendations: If you are not already, I would expect that you are going to ask for recommendations. You can increase your marketing results by up to 4 times through your past work, through referrals. This is something that should be mentioned at the onset of your business process with any of your client's transactions. Additionally, an honest review is something you should always ask for.

Your Structure and Consistency: the best way to succeed is to build a great system. It adds to a consistent and structured environment that will be at your fingertips. What I mean by this is such things as having templates in place for every letter or communication scenario. This way, you are not missing anything important and the reach-outs to your clients are always consistent. When you have standard forms on file, you come across as organized, structured and professional.

"Give them quality. That's the best kind of advertising" – Milton Hershey

Look ahead: We are all concerned with when our next commission comes in and what it looks like, but have you thought far enough ahead to know what your next several years' revenue will look like? You always want to be thinking about how you get yourself to stand out from the crowd and why your next clients would choose you over so many other options. If you are always keeping that top of mind, you will find your niche within a market of many, that has you above the crowd, with people blowing up your phone!

CHAPTER 3

Dreaded Cold Calls – New Clients

Now comes the feared part of the business which is safe to collectively say, cold calling and those follow-up calls from open houses. Some agents may be comfortable with these methods of drumming up business, while others don't like this part of building a client base and building the business. Either way, this is an important part of this business and if not the absolute most important part of your business development. And trust me, without it, you will fail before you even start. Unfortunately, there are not a lot of agents that have the money to hit the ground running with fancy marketing and signage to help boost their exposure and increase a client base.

This is why without cold calling and door knocking, not much lucrative opportunity will happen. Here is where you will develop a great part of your character in real estate. It takes a thick skin to be able to handle some of the rejection and what can be negative responses that come with this part of starting off in real estate, which is not any different than opening and starting your own business from scratch. It's a tough gig, but honestly, very worthwhile.

"Everything You've Ever Wanted Is On The Other Side Of Fear" – George Addair

I talk with my own staff often about just this, because rejection and dead ends can be discouraging. Keeping positive, taking a deep breath before making a call and after a negative call, stand up and walk it off; these are all suggestions that I give to my own team! You can't let it define your day, or your day is over before it starts. Refuse to let it beat you down, because without these calls and the face-to-face meetings, there is no business. I can assure you that you will eventually get *THAT* call that turns everything around, wait for it!

As a novice, or even a seasoned agent, whenever you get someone that is a warm lead, you should quickly take the opportunity to ask if you can drop by their home; seize the moment. Use the opportunity to get some face-to-face experience and get some time in talking with some potential clients. It may seem like a waste of time, gas and efforts, but if you don't do this, you won't get the feel for talking with people and getting familiar with the entire process. You can let them know that you know their area and feel it may be worth a conversation, whether this is the case or not. Then you need to do your homework and make the conversation worthwhile.

You should always treat a potential client with sincere respect and deep interest. If you are going to take the time to see someone, don't waste the opportunity to build a trusting relationship. If you end up dazzling them in the end, whether you get the listing or not, you've just started the gradual process of networking and relationship building and you never know who will pass along your business card or recommend you as a result. And that you will find is a reliable source of business. The referral!

I highly recommend using a script when cold calling. The reason I have for this is that the process of cold calling can be intimidating, as we already know, and if you get someone that is less than pleasant on the end of the line, that can escalate the intimidation factor, leaving you uncomfortably stumbling over your words and you might miss saying something. So, if you have something in black and white, right in front of you, with points to share with the caller, then you can stay focused and keep the call short and to the point if need be.

Here's a tip that helped me and my agents over the years — before you pick up the phone, get out of your own head. This is especially true for new agents. You only need to prove that you know what you're doing and that you are a professional. Your posture and confidence are crucial to getting the person on the other end of the line to let their guard down and start telling you about where they are or if they are considering selling their property anytime soon.

Here is a short, non-offensive, yet effective script to use when cold calling:

"Hello, I am calling because my company has buyers looking for a home in your neighborhood. Are you thinking of selling soon?"

Making cold calls to homeowners who are confused by the reason for your call — why you are calling — is a waste of your time. You want the homeowner to understand instantly and clearly why you are calling.

Another bit of advice is when using this sample script above, or any script in real estate, it's best to always pause after the words "real estate." Something along the lines of this; "Hi, this is Annie Nickerson from ABC Realty. (breath…) I am calling because…"

The reason you want to be deliberate about the pause is that it gives the caller a moment to understand why you are calling. Always assume that people are in the middle of their own life when you interject with a call. The slight pause in the conversation will avoid any confusion on their end as to the reason for your call.

Even when you answer a phone call, it takes a few seconds to absorb the spoken word, so they know who the caller is. Once they know who you are, and they know the call is about real estate, suddenly, the homeowner's mind is prepared for a call about, well, real estate.

Keep in mind that the goal of a cold call is not to close a deal, but to open a door to a client or a potential client. Establish a new relationship, this is what a new real estate professional needs the most of when starting off.

Another reasonable way of connecting with potential business in real estate is through your existing contacts. These are people that you have accumulated incidentally over the years like friends, family and acquaintances. Nothing is too big or too small and you never know who is sitting in their living room at night evaluating their life, or property situation, considering upsizing or downsizing for that matter.

I will bet you have access to a surprising bevy of contacts right at your fingertips! And these contacts are certainly some you could and should be using.

One thing that I hear the most from new real estate agents is that they do not know any creative ideas to find their first seller client. It seems like finding buyer clients is easy and that many agents are intimidated by having to find listing clients. Here are some solid ways to find listings.

First, let's consider how sellers pick listing agents. There is an old saying that "buyers buy houses and sellers buy marketing" and there is truth here! Your potential listing only wants two things, to sell fast for the most money possible. To do this, often, they think that an agent with a high profile can help and sometimes this is true, but not always.

But what if you do not have any listings to show off yet? Guess what, do a brochure and underscore your skills. This worked for me in the early days, I do recommend it. You can order just the smallest amount at first, and I must say that having that business card gave me the self-confidence I needed to approach sellers.

How about you ask your colleagues to borrow your listings. There are people around you who have listings who would love to have open houses, amazing pictures or free promotions. Borrow listings to use in your marketing that target the same types of sellers that you would like to work with.

You want to spend a significant amount of time researching your neighborhoods, finding out about the market and knowing your stuff. Now, you do not have to memorize any of these things, but you should have a great understanding of what is going on in your area and the neighborhood of your listing appointment.

Here is a daily challenge for you, get **five** names of people into your database <u>every day</u>. This will help to determine your success. This is what will help you have leads to follow up on down the line. So, who are these people you will be adding? Friends, family, people at the gym, past work-mates, the attendant at the drycleaners, whomever.

Once you have people in your database, you want to start emailing them at least once a week. This does not have to be difficult, you can just do a little message about a new listing that came on the market, a household tip or even a recipe if that is how you roll.

The biggest problem I have seen with people's list over time is that they think they need to wait until they have an accumulation of people to message or that they are afraid of "bothering" them. You need to message them weekly, right off the top. Just send something interesting so they know that you are going to be actively reaching out to them.

Some people do this automatically by having a "drip marketing campaign" which is just a series of emails that goes out once a person signs up. Do not make this hard; it can be as simple as explaining parts of the real estate process to first time seller prospects or fun facts about your local town or city.

I don't expect that all these options will appeal to you. How about you start by picking one or two to focus on and then get to work and get your first client!

Now, let's consider what to do with leads. Once you start doing some of the marketing that I am going to suggest, you will start to get leads for listings and the saddest thing in the world would be to let them all go to waste.

Friends & family: It is really tempting to try and avoid "bothering" your friends and family when you get into real estate, but they can be a source of some of your early listings. I added everyone I knew to my database after asking them if it was okay to send them info from time to time. Full disclosure and permission are always best so as not to annoy and get people's backs up. Here is an example of what I have said and what you many want to consider saying:

"I am excited to share with you that I've finally received my real estate licence. I am trying to build up my list of people who might refer me clients and I am asking for your **help** in growing my business. I would be grateful to be able to add your name to my contact list. Do you mind? I will only send you amazing info and this would be extremely helpful!

It's not rocket science, you simply have to ask the question. Don't overthink it and you'll grow your contact base. It is a bit frightening initially, but most people do want to help you. I suggest you use the word "help me." It is human nature to want to help. And I personally did ask everyone I met when I first started, and as a matter of fact, I still do!

Now, here are different ways to get listings or leads:

- ***Expired:*** I do see value in expired listings. These are the people who at one point wanted to sell, and they did hire a listing agent. So, if handled correctly, they should be easy to convert. You want to take the time and do your research. There could be a few obvious reasons for the expired listing; pictures were not good, description was not great, or they were simply overpriced. What you do once you have come to a reasonable conclusion is call them or quickly visit if you cannot get a number. Be mindful that lots of agents will be contacting them; having a bit of insight into their home and why it did not sell will go a long way.

- ***For sale by owner listings:*** I'm not overly thrilled about FSBO targeting because I simply don't want to justify the legitimacy of Realtors to the person who feels they can sell their own home. Overall, FSBOs are a more difficult group to work with but this is a practical resource for business. If a certain amount of time goes by and FSBO listing is still on the market, you will find the sellers become more open to entertaining the idea of listing with a certified real estate agent.

- ***Website:*** Unfortunately, many agents are not internet savvy, but if you are, then you have an advantage right off the hop. You should have something along the lines of an email popup on your site and try to get sellers on your list by giving them free guides like, "10 of the Best Things To Do Prior To Listing Your Home" and "Why Overestimating Your Home's Worth Can Cost You In The End."

Open House: I believe that <u>open houses</u> are the easiest way to get leads. I do my open houses, Monday through Thursday from 5-7, and of course a weekend open house is always effective. If someone stops at your open house after working all day and before getting dinner on the table, they are doing real estate soon.

Open houses are usually manned by buyers' agents who are typically annoyed that the "meddlesome neighbors" are the majority of the ones coming in and I say to that attitude "what?!" Those meddlesome neighbors are listing opportunities in the making. They can act as your best marketing agents and they can and will talk up or down the house you are in. Let them know you have researched the neighborhood and seize the opportunity and offer to pop by and let them know what the market is doing in their neighborhood and let them know what their home may be worth. Even if they tell you that they are not selling for a couple of years, just let them know that there are things they should and shouldn't do. Let them know you are an expert and be super helpful and you might be surprised by what can come from it. They are thinking of selling in under a year or just over a year, with or without you.

Stay connected with these hot listing leads and do the extra work now to make sure they remember you.

- ***Facebook & Instagram live:*** As I've said before, I think that this is one of the most effective innovative marketing channels that are out there. Having a "live" from an open house opportunity while previewing a listing or even just highlighting an area is a way to generate interest from potential sellers and buyers. Opening your phone once a day and detailing what you are up to is a fantastic way to get exposure for your business.

The reason it is so effective right now, is that Facebook and Instagram will notify your followers on these social media platforms when you are live, and then they will promote the recording a fair amount after it ends, it's brilliant. This is much more effective than just posting aimlessly on social media.

YouTube Videos: This is becoming the future of marketing. People rarely take the time to read a 3,000 word blog post or even a quick email message, but they are using YouTube to find out about goods and services in their area. Again, this is a brilliant tool to utilize and you can make it somewhat fun and still professional as well, who knows, it could become your branding outlet. As a listing agent, you can stake claim to any neighborhood you like, simply by taking neighborhood videos of the amenities, sample houses, parks and schools (off hours of course) and the like. You can also become a recognized expert in your town or area easily by taking people on "tour" videos and talking about what is interesting about your neighborhood. The options for the creative real estate agent are endless.

- ***Networking:*** We have touched on the "creative" marketing ideas. Now let's go back to the old school networking. That said, you want to be very targeted in who you are networking with. Here are a few people that could help your listings get off the ground fast. Realtors. Yep, many listing agents will not list properties under a certain amount or if they are too far away from their office. Also consider people who work for sellers, such as handymen/women, landscapers and painters. All of these are good networking opportunities.

- *Referrals:* Most people are not great at selling, and especially at selling themselves. Thus, you will need to make sure it's super easy for friends and family to refer you out. I recommend using business cards with your picture or logo on the front and then a "referred by" line on the back. You can give 5 of them to your best clients and let them know when you get a referral from them, you will send out a special gift (a $5-15 Starbucks card is a suggestion). Do not worry about whether you get a client or not, reward them every time they recommend someone to you, you want to have a constant stream of people ringing your phone because something will pan out eventually.

  This act of giving them a gift makes them feel like they are "helping" as I mentioned earlier, people innately want to help. And in turn, they get a bonus gift thanking them for the referral. It keeps a momentum going that will motivate them to "help" you over and over. As an additional bonus, when you are sending out a newsletter, make sure to put a "Refer a Friend" section in there and put in a call out to everyone who sent you a referral that month. This is so effective in promotion of "refer a friend."

- *Door knocking:* Door knocking in your neighborhood of choice is a great idea. You can get to know potential clients, ask them if they would like monthly updates and generally make friends with the homeowners. I always remember people who have shown up at my door when I get a flyer in the mail from them. It's a great way to put yourself out there. Talk about their lovely flowers, great landscaping, or fantastic location. Get them to understand that you're a detail-oriented person and you have a sincere interest in their home.

Additionally, don't miss the opportunity to leave your contact information. That being said, I think you should have something to give them. Try something like a sheet with a list of local tradespeople, the schools and emergency numbers and of course, your contact information in case they need a great real estate agent in the future. You might want to consider having this sheet on coloured paper and laminate it; as this is your area of business anyway, you'll use them frequently. Laminated paper gives the illusion of value and is less likely to be thrown away.

"Keep Yourself Positive, Cheerful And Goal-Oriented. Sales Success Is 80% Attitude And Only 20% Aptitude" – Brian Tracy

CHAPTER 4

Be Positive

The other day I was discussing business practices with some colleagues and it occurred to me that of all the characteristics that someone could possibly possess, being positive will take you the furthest both professionally and personally. Part of being positive is showing up and making things happen without letting feelings like rejection interfere in your positive energy. It's just a reality that rejection will happen. You can allow it to bring you down <u>or</u> you allow yourself the freedom to know that, it is what it is and move on.

I have hired some seasoned real estate agents over the years. As you could imagine, I was excited to bring them and their experience into my brokerage. I truly felt honoured as I thought it would be dynamic new energy, full of great opportunities with an amazing knowledge base. Unfortunately, that didn't turn out to be the case, as they were in fact, not very positive people, they were the reverse of positive. They came carrying baggage and real cynicism. They were opposing and seemingly contaminated by their years in Real Estate. They possessed nothing except for a lackluster attitude, which stunned and disappointed me.

This experience gave me pause to always have a re-think about the kind of people I bring into my team, and more so, surround myself with. So, I decided that I would have to select my circle a little more considerately. I decided to create a positive environment and hire a team that reflected my positive attitude and atmosphere as well. The moral of the story here is, the most positive group of people you can find to surround yourself with is key to a happy, productive life, both inside and outside of real estate.

It turns out that whether you're a seasoned real estate agent or a novice one, if you don't have the right attitude of gratitude, you are not going to find sales in this industry very rewarding. Attitude is not something you can learn from a book, it's a way of thinking. We all have bad days, but I strongly suggest that you fake it until you make it, because it will serve you well in the long run.

Imagine walking into an office and being greeted by a particularly irritable individual, the tone of the meeting is set. You can permit it to dictate the balance of the interaction or you can be the person to turn that around or at least the person that tries to spin it on a brighter axis. It takes optimism and a positive attitude to know that you can make a difference not only in your own day, but also in someone else's day. This is how we should all start our day off. *Choose to be positive today.* Say that to yourself when you wake up and maybe 20 other times throughout the day, whenever you need the boost, which will be often. The truth is that sometimes life will interfere and at times an unhappy person may be fighting a real battle we are not aware of, so the key to success in your day-to-day life both professional and personal, is to be positive and always be kind.

We affect, and are affected by the people we meet, in one way or another. This happens instinctively and on an inadvertent level, through words, thoughts and feelings, and a lot through our communication both verbal and of our body language.

It's not a wonder that we tend to gravitate towards positive people, and prefer to avoid negative ones. People are more likely to help us, if we are positive, and they have an aversion and avoid anyone spewing any kind of negativity. This is just the rule of being human.

Negative thoughts, words and attitude create negative and unhappy feelings, moods and behavior. It's a slippery slope of dissemination. When the mind is negative, toxins are released into the blood and further into your dopamine-producing ability, which cause more grief and pessimism. This will not typically end in your favour.

Follow some of these tips for attracting positive people into your life…

Trash the news: Because the news really is trash. This may appear to be an unrealistic expectation, but it's an important one. I have had many people tell me this over the years, and here it is, stop watching, listening to or reading the news. Yes, really! The news is based on negativity, it feeds on fear and despair to capture its audience. Media is a business like anything else and there's a saying, bad news sells, good news just doesn't sell as well.

This heightened fear-based information highway is what helps to keep negativity streaming through our veins. Joyful and positive doesn't sell newspapers or attract the internet or television viewers the way fear-based propaganda does.

"One reason that cats are happier than people are that they have no newspapers"
— **Gwendolyn Brooks, In the Mecca**

Second, stop being around negative people when at all possible. Colleagues are going to want to tell you how bad the state of the world is, or maybe your clients or future clients are going to say how bad it is, and perhaps friends will do the same thing. You may want to deter this line of conversation.

- ***Try to avoid negative and adverse people*** and if you can't avoid them, then please don't become them. You can do things such as change the subject, change the conversation so they stop talking about one topic and on to the next. I refer to these negative people as people who are "comfortable with chaos." It's actually fairly easy to do once you get into the habit of pushing away the negativity of the nay-sayers. It's not long before people stop talking about topics that have an unwelcome effect on your psyche. These "comfortable with chaos" people likely won't stop all together, and that's okay if you define the parameters of what you'll tolerate and what you won't tolerate. They will eventually get the message and move along and probably talk negative to other people, but not you and that's acceptable.

- ***Thought stopping is another effective technique***. The first step is just to catch yourself thinking thoughts that bring you down. It's a present moment awareness that you must become mindful of at any given moment. It's an easy process once you train yourself to become cognisant of the thoughts to begin with. Once you catch yourself in the negative thoughts, you simply stop.

  It really **is** that easy. The more you do it, the better you get, the more conscious you become and the quicker you learn to reverse the thoughts.

Here's the thing, we all self-talk and unfortunately, we are all our own worst enemies and our own harshest critics. We say stuff to ourselves like; "I just don't have what it takes to be effective or I don't have what it takes to make the kind of money that such and such makes," or "Things don't come easy for me" or "why did I do this?", or "why did I say that?" It's up to you to catch those negative thoughts as early as you can once the thought arises in your mind, right in the beginning. And reverse the inner voice to "I can and will be successful or I did the best I could in the situation." "Maybe I shouldn't have said that," and "I learned from it, I will do better next time." Replace it with a positive new thought and let go of the negative old thought. Those old thoughts are NOT doing you any good.

Humans are said to have somewhere in the neighbourhood of 60,000 thoughts a day, but unfortunately, they are the same 60,000 thoughts as we had yesterday. Change the conversation in your head.

New thoughts are easy to replace old thoughts with, and you can speak to the negative one entering your mind at any given moment. Such as in Real estate, it might be something along the lines of "I'm not good enough or experienced enough to close this deal, or get this listing" to something along the lines of "I have studied hard and I am smart and capable, and the experience will come every time I get a listing and sell a home, just like everyone else in this industry." You have these and many alternative ways to draw from your existing positive thought pool.

"Believing in negative thoughts is the single greatest obstruction to success"
— **Charles F. Glassman, <u>Brain Drain The Breakthrough That Will Change Your Life</u>**

Think about some of the things you've learned over time and the successes you've had since you were very young. Did you learn to ride a bike without training wheels or play hockey in a team environment? You may or may not remember, but you didn't know how to do that before you started! It's no different as we get older, the only difference is that we tend to hold onto things more as we get older, especially negative memories and thoughts and we've allowed the world to damage us without knowing it. The self-defeating conversations in our heads are louder as we age, and we believe them more than when we were children. This is problematic because it holds us back with fear and we believe that negative and destructive voice.

When you catch yourself thinking something like, "I've failed," look closely at the thought and try to be specific: *Did you fail or did your plan of action fail*? Beliefs are something that you continually tell yourself: "In order to succeed, I'll have to work 20 hours a day, and there goes my life." If that's been your main belief, use thought stopping, and change the conversation in your head to, "Nope, I'm not going there. I'm just not going there." An alternative positive thought could then be, "I'm going to find a way to work smart and be home with my family more. I'm going to work smarter, not harder."

One of the things that's great about this practice is that it really forces you to become aware of what you're thinking from moment to moment, and it's what you're thinking from moment to moment that will create a negative or positive mindset and literally dictate how your day, week or month unfolds. If you're repeatedly thinking negative thoughts about yourself or the environment you are in, or about money, or about your relationship, the kids or any situation, then you're going to continue the path of a negative mindset, it's just the law of the universe. Then what happens has a tendency to come true, it's a slippery slope and becomes a self-fulfilling prophecy. You create the self-fulfilling prophecy by repeatedly telling yourself the same things whether negative OR positive. You can decide, you do decide, make a different decision today.

You can't always control what goes on outside of you, but you absolutely can control what goes on inside your mind. You need to have unyielding faith in your ability to be successful. The way you do that is to retrain your mind, retrain your thoughts. The thought-stopping practice is the most powerful tool for retraining your mind, but be warned, you may have to use it a few hundred times a day at the beginning. Don't be impatient with yourself at the start of this process and retraining. It took many years of negative self-talk to get to where you are, it will take time to become the person you know you can become.

It really is just a matter of; "If you change the way you look at things, the things you look at change" — Wayne Dyer.

Having a positive mindset has been identified through numerous studies to a mentally, physically, and emotionally healthy lifestyle and individual. It's also worth mentioning that the most successful people in any given industry are often the ones who can keep a positive outlook. Being a real estate professional is tough, no doubt. And in this industry, it is easy to feel over-extended, burned out, or pessimistic. For real estate professionals, it's therefore doubly important to be deliberate about crafting an optimistic mindset.

Self-care is important to maintaining a positive attitude. Day-to-day life as a real estate professional can be jam-packed, intense and stressful. In times of stress, many of us inadvertently end up working even harder or putting in even more hours. While a strong work ethic is a great thing, it is also important to remember to allow yourself time to step away from the grind. Many people unintentionally wear themselves down, never giving themselves a chance to mend. If you find your stress is through the roof, allow yourself permission to step away from the grind and take care of yourself. After a short rest, you will be able to take on anything with a refreshed enthusiasm.

Eliminate negative self-talk. "I can't do it," your inner voice tells you. "This isn't going well," or "I always screw up." To some degree or another, everyone on the planet deals with prevalent negative self-thoughts. Unfortunately, it can be extremely easy to dwell on the negativity, especially in such a high performance-based field as real estate.

The first step in crafting a positive outlook is to transform those negative self-doubts into statements of positive intention or positive affirmations. To some, this may sound quirky, but give it a chance, it does work! When you start thinking, "I can't do this," instead say, "I will work to see this through, regardless." Whatever your insecurity, doubt or fear, when it creeps into your conscious mind, it reveals itself, and then you have the power to flip it on its head.

One of the best ways to maintain a positive mindset is to set realistic goals, and then commit to seeing them through. Your work ethic could be stellar, week in and week out and you are putting in maximum effort, and yet at the end of the month, you still feel as if you haven't gotten where you wanted to be. Setting goals is a great way to be able to see the concrete results of your hard work, and when you can see how far you've come, it is easier to stay motivated. As you surpass your goals, you can take pride in your progress, and that in turn boosts your confidence. This will only project you to further achieve your goals and noticeable success. That's exactly how it works, set a goal, achieve and believe, then rinse and repeat.

The people that we surround ourselves with, have an incredible impact on the way we think and feel. Validation is sought by negative people for their own lack of success or lack of confidence or overall dissatisfaction, from whoever is around them. In other words, misery loves company. Unfortunately, it's very easy to get caught up in the drama of negativity and it's also easy to let it bring you down. Therefore, the trick is to stay clear of the negative and surround yourself with positive upbeat individuals. They will be the ones that will motivate you to greater personal heights. Keeping a positive outlook on life, accomplishment and joy can and do often go hand in hand.

In some circles, it is said that the most successful people are up at the crack of dawn and start their morning with either reading, meditation, jogging or something that gives their day purpose and a fresh start with a clear and stimulated mind. Whatever that looks like for you, just do it. And don't forget, be kind and be positive.

"Attitude is a choice. Happiness is a choice. Optimism is a choice. Kindness is a choice. Giving is a choice. Respect is a choice. Whatever choice you make, makes you. Choose wisely" — Roy T. Bennett

So many real estate professionals today are wondering, "How can I stay positive in today's market, in today's financial climate, with so many obligations and so much stress?" Like any discerning real estate professional, you realize the value of a positive mental attitude. Here are some ways that you can create and maintain a positive mental attitude.

- *Avoid toxic people:* What does this mean and who are the toxic people? Toxic people can be well-meaning, well-intentioned people but they are coming from a negative attitude about things like money, finances, and perhaps about the current real estate situation.

  They may be fellow real estate professionals who want to gather around the water cooler, they may be relatives who are just trying to protect you; they may even be friends and family. You will know if you've been around a toxic person, because you will begin to feel deflated and even fatigued.

"You cannot expect to live a positive life if you hang with negative people" — **Joel Osteen**

Here's how you should handle this negative proximity, either change the subject or walk away. Better yet, speak up for yourself and tell them that you want to think positively about yourself and about your business. If you see one of them coming your way, find a way to avoid the contact because it does not serve your highest good or theirs for that matter.

Failing that and doing all that you can do to protect yourself from the constricts of the negative thinkers, consider some more of these suggestions below:

- **Develop an inner mantra.** You can do this by simply having your own inner conversation if someone is saying something negative to you on the outside. A great example of an inner conversation when someone is complaining about their business or about the marketplace is to say to yourself, "That may be true for you but it's not true for me." Make this or something similar your inner mantra. You are the only one that can make a difference for *you*, so you have nothing to lose.

- **Successful real estate professionals do well in any market.**

  Were you aware of that? Knowing that fact, none of us can continue to use the excuse about the market being bad. In addition to the right marketing strategies and regular lead-generation activities and among many of the suggested tips throughout this book, you could also help yourself with this empowered belief and mantra:

"I draw clients to myself who are ready, willing and able to make a transaction in the next 30 days."

• ***Look for the opportunity.***

There are many opportunities in today's market and successful real estate professionals are taking advantage of them. Let your prospective clients know this and then say to them, "Let's get you a deal." Few could resist this invitation.

• ***Your success depends on your mindset.***

What mindset do you choose to nurture inside yourself? Do you want to believe, "I can "or "I can't"? Your beliefs create your reality so whatever you choose to believe will become true for you. Here's a tip: instead of saying "I can't possibly succeed in today's market," choose instead to focus on positive beliefs, like "I achieve whatever I set my mind to."

"If you believe you can or you can't, either way you are right" — *Henry Ford.*

• ***Be proactive***

In any business climate, there are always people wanting to buy and sell homes. That's the beauty of this industry. They need your help and they need your knowledge. Your job is to become visible to them and the reality is that they are not likely to fall into your lap. However, with a good system of lead generation, you can contact them and use your intention to attract your ideal clients. Remove any self-limiting beliefs that stop you from picking up the phone.

Follow the suggestions mentioned above and you'll be happy to notice that you are not only staying more positive, but also your income is increasing as well.

"Life is 10% what happens to us and 90% how we react to it" – Dennis P. Kimbro

CHAPTER 5

Your Mindset is Your Success

Your mindset is established set of attitudes

Now this established mindset can and is often easily changed. Either you embrace it or you don't but the reality is of determining your mindset and putting it into action. If you study things that are outside your current mindset, then you can change it. That is how people evolve. It's been said that your mindset is your most important asset. How you think your life is turning out and what you think of the world at any given moment, these are mindsets. Positive or negative, forward thinking or retrospective, these are the questions you need to ask yourself. Which are you?

It seems to me that a lot of people say that they want certain things out of their life, as such is their mindset. For example, the dream job, the great home, the marriage, the sports car, whatever, but in reality they don't actually want what they say they want. Because guess what? It's simply too hard to develop and adhere to a process of thinking, and then acting to have all of these great things. In other words, you must position yourself and do the work to get your mindset aligned with your actions, into a state of congruence.

In order to help you with that congruent attitude or mindset, you'll find a few things to help you along this road. First thing you need to do is to *identify your purpose.* What is it that you are here on this earth for? What is it that you are wanting to achieve from your life? What makes you happy? These are not questions that you can answer after a few minutes of consideration. They are deep methodical questions that you have to ask yourself again and again, and get to the real depth of who you are in order to answer. And once you are truly able to identify your purpose, then you have to go inward again and figure out exactly how hard you're willing to work to get what you want.

So, let's examine this a little further. What is it that you feel is your calling in life, whether you look at your current or future career or you look at your family or your friend base? What does your life look like in 5 or 10 years from now? Are you just a real estate agent? Are you a successful real estate agent? Or are you a Million Dollar Agent? Are you wanting material goals such as a new car or a new house, or are you searching for respect and influence? What exactly is it that you aspire for? Which one of these questions speak to you and which one rings the truest? If you're an agent, that's great. If you're a Million Dollar Agent, that's great too. What are you doing to make your mindset or belief reflect that?

You mindset is something that resonates deeply within your purpose and once you are easily able to identify your purpose, you start to do something called *creating vision.*

How do you envision yourself? Let's talk real estate, let's get to the fundamental meat and potatoes of the industry. Do you have the hunter mindset? Is it an established set of attitudes that brings success? When people ask you how you get your business, does this mindset come out loud and proud? Such as, *I am a hunter and I make 20 calls a day to potential clients!* Or are you a little more sheepish with that question, and cringe at the question because you know it's your weakness and that you are happy to actually make 5 calls a week because you let something that you strongly dislike, paralyze you?

If you are either a hunter or if prospecting paralyses you, just know that it's a mindset and a belief. The good news is that your mindset can be changed. Whatever you want to aspire to achieve, you quite literally have to change your mindset and your beliefs to reflect the success you want to achieve. This may sound complicated but it's actually not complicated. The good news is that a mindset is a choice, mindsets are just beliefs. The idea behind changing a mindset to give you an advantage in the world of real estate success, is exciting.

Next, you should consider *ignoring your critics while you are fighting your own negativity.* People will always try to dissuade you from your thinking especially if you're trying to improve on yourself or your business. They may even chastise or criticize you; let them but don't let them win.

You have to remain strong in your thoughts and convictions, don't let the voices of the few take you from your objectives. It's easy to say but you'll find over time this is more about the commitment you make to yourself than it is the good opinions of others that quite frankly shouldn't have a say in your life. One way to avoid this is, making sure you don't share what you are doing with others. Maybe you share your desire to change with your spouse or partner or someone you know will support and encourage you. Otherwise, the good opinion of others, is not your business. Think about that statement while you travel through this journey to self-improvement.

I'll tell you that there are only a select few that I have ever let into my personal goals. What this did for me was give me the room to grow in my mindset and beliefs. And the changes were without justification. It was liberating to have made some real internal progress without the critics attempting to pull me down.

Let's change gears now with a question to consider. What is it that sets those who accomplish great things apart from those who fail to realize their dreams? You might suspect one's aptitude, perhaps even imagination. Reasonable suggestions, right? But the science says something different. The supporting information below was found from the following: www.inc.com/jessica-stillman/5-steps-to-get-the-right-mindset-for-success.html.

According to a research work by pioneering Stanford psychologist Carol Dweck and others, "the best predictor of success in life is none of these usual suspects—it's your mindset." Those who realize levels of success in life do this because they believe that they can. This is called a "growth mindset." People who have failed attempts at certain levels of success have a mindset that renders them unable to achieve success. In other words, they have a fixed mindset.

Identifying this is very interesting and it begs the question — if up till now you've believed you were unchangeable through a fixed mindset, can you change? Unquestionably, start learning to view your capabilities as ever evolving, and unlearning your fixed beliefs.

Below are some suggestions to help you do this:

- A mindset will develop over many years. I refer throughout this book about the conversation that we carry on in our own heads, for better and sometimes for worse. Once you identify this is happening, it can illuminate where you can start to change the way you look at yourself and your beliefs. Think about how you've handled situations outside of your comfort zone in the past. That voice might say to you, what makes you think you can do this? What makes you think you've got the aptitude? However, as you hit an impediment, the voice in your head might say, "This would have been a snap if you really had talent." Ah the self-denigrating talk!

Pay attention to your thoughts and see if you frequently tell yourself anything similar. If so, you've spotted the fixed mindset at work, deflating the likeliness for your success.

Growth mindset is now a possibility, now you can change the conversation in your head to something a little less limiting. When should you do this and how should you do this? Well it is fairly simple. Now that you know the different beliefs we hold and how they affect our abilities to grow or not, you have the decision to make as to how you will deal with these mindsets. "How you interpret challenges, setbacks, and criticism is your choice," the post points out. "You can interpret them in a fixed mindset as signs that your fixed talents or abilities are lacking. Or you can interpret them in a growth mindset as signs that you need to ramp up your strategies and effort, stretch yourself, and expand your abilities."

Upon hearing that voice reflecting a fixed mindset in your head, be aggressive with it in the process of retraining. Start adding some positive language to your responses and redirect that voice to an all-knowing and all possibilities framework, including your new growth mindset. The difference would be something along the line of fixed mindset, "You don't have the talent to pull that off" to growth mindset, "You can do it, it will take time and some time and determination, but you can do it." The difference is profound in how your life can and will unfold.

Now you've identified that there is a narrative in your head that needs to change before you can grow. Keep in mind, the point to this potentially life-changing exercise is that now you have to incorporate the change into a modification in your behaviour. It doesn't end at realizing that your voice needs to be different, you have to have your actions reflect that voice. Get out there and practice what you're preaching to yourself.

Here are some effects of mindsets to be wary of in your thought processes.

Having said the above about the wonderful and real process of mindset re-framing, it's also cautionary to understand that this is not without reasonable restrictions. Here is a statement to consider while you read on. It's always a possibility to advance in your mindset; however, it is not always possible for you to reach a specific achievement.

Here's a rather abstract example, but you probably get the point. Let's say you have always dreamed of being a doctor, but you literally vomit every time you see blood, you can almost be assured that your dreams even with a change in mindset will not materialize. Here's the thing, you believe you should be capable of literally everything, unfortunately, many people end up thinking that, and then they waste their efforts in what ends up being acts of self-deception.

This caution and disclaimer of sorts is really important for disabled people. It might be true that if you worked hard, then you would improve your driving skills, but if you have certain disabilities for example, like impaired vision, it might also be true that no matter how hard you work, you'll never be a safe driver.

It's not fixed mindset to say, given my limitations, it's dangerous for me to be on the road, and it will no longer be how hard I work at driving. It's common sense.

Another thing to consider, just because you *can* improve something doesn't mean you *ought to*. Let's consider something like motor skills. My ability to type isn't the strongest. In fact, I'm a one-fingered typist and having said that, I could in fact take some classes and improve my speed and accuracy. But should I do this given my very busy life? Not really necessary as my work requires little typing and seeking classes for such a thing is not to advantage at this point in my life.

Here is the thing with this scenario that with enough effort, people can improve just about anything. However, it might be that the required energy is arbitrary for you right now (you might not have the spare time to go to typing classes). It might be that improving at that skill requires more effort for you than for most people and it just isn't always reasonable to consider changing a mindset or behaviour.

The bottom line with this is that it's actually quite empowering to think or to say out loud, "I can improve, but I don't want to or need to at this point. I have the option to do what I want to increase my personal station in life. The decision to do or not to do, is mine and mine alone. If I'm not good at something, I can decide to put effort into it without thinking but I'm so awful at this, *I shouldn't waste my time*, or *I can decide to skip it without thinking but other people can do this! I should be able to as well.* If I'm good at something, I can decide to put effort into it without thinking *I'm already okay at this, I should stop wasting my time trying to get better*, and I can decide to skip it without thinking I'm wasting my potential."

Another way to think as to any of the above fixed ways of thinking, simply add the word, *yet*. For example*, I can't do this task, yet*. Rather than, *I can't do this task*. See how this ups the internal dialogue to something that is more positive to your inner script.

Ultimately, there are lots of things I could improve in my life such as, gardening, poetry writing, painting, etc. but what do I actually want to spend my time improving? This is what you have to determine. What about your needs to change so that you can better do what your purpose is, in the most effective way possible?

Once you get that question answered, you can then move forward with unnecessary energy, likely in the real-estate industry. That would make the most sense.

Of course, you are an adult and you get to make your *own* decisions about what you do or don't improve in your life. Other people may certainly get to object or even stop talking to you as a result, but ultimately it's none of their business what you choose to improve, or not improve for that matter.

If you're around a person like that, feel free to say *I can't* whenever you mean *I have done the cost/benefit analysis and it is not worth it*. Growth mindset is an inner and very personal journey to re-frame thinking and actions that doesn't have to be applied to or explained to a persona non grata.

CHAPTER 6

Mindset in Business

What are the effects of mindset on starting and growing your own business? The reality is it can impact your business a great deal, in ways you might not have even imagined. Through the years, I have seen changes in mindset that has taken place not only within myself, but a few key people that I have business associations with. Not only myself but the others I am referring to have experienced such things as creative blocks and the overall inability to move forward because of self-inflicted barriers. Having the right mindset in your business is about how you function within your business to encourage business growth and success. In real estate, we need to be aware that if you are fragile in your mindset, the results could be devastating.

Below are some ways in which mindset can affect your business.

Creativity can be affected. This can have some negative impacts on your business as it deals with marketing and sales and overall business strategies. If you have a creative block, you will find that the ability to think outside the box isn't as easy as it should be. In real estate, it is so important to be original as there are lots of agents out there. What will make you stand out from the crowd if you don't have the muscle to think creatively?

Creativity simply cannot flourish when you are stuck in a fixed mindset. Sometimes clients say to me, *I can't* or *I don't know what to do.* The truth is, they don't know what to do YET. The beauty of this is, with the right support and resources, it is possible to change thinking, become *unstuck* and work out the best way forward. I'm a great believer in our potential only being limited by our mindset.

Resilience: We've all heard the memes that infers *failure is the key to success.* What does this actually mean in real life? The failure itself is not the key, what you learn from it and how you grow and evolve. 80% of businesses don't actually fail — 80% of business owners burn out.

How do you know it's time to shake up your mindset? When you're feeling a bit like a mouse on a wheel — expending loads of energy and not getting anywhere. This is where burn-out begins to occur and it can happen at any stage of business. Being able to utilize your mindset to overcome failure, obstacles and adversity, to find the learning curve and apply it in new and creative ways to move forward is critical. As mentioned above, those who have developed a *growth mindset* are more likely to value the learning than despair over the failure.

Accountability: When you are your own boss, no one can hold you accountable but yourself. This can lead to a tendency for procrastination. I've coached clients who have a lot of great ideas and are struggling to implement them, which was leading to poor sales and failing businesses. To add insult to injury for them, sometimes they would procrastinate about their need to tackle their procrastination!

Procrastination in and of itself can be complex. If it is hindering the growth of your business, it's important to think about what assistance and resources you might need to help you move past it. I've worked with clients who have been able to develop tools and strategies that they've continued to successfully use after our coaching program finished. One client wrote to me to tell me how she has been using our tools and strategies in her everyday life, which I thought was brilliant!

Perfectionism: I've worked with clients whose perfectionism was driving them to physical exhaustion. It would manifest in different ways from feeling unable to let go of or pass work on, over-commitment, and a series of hasty decisions out of fear of making the wrong decision (which inevitably lead them into one mighty pickle).

One example of how you can stifle the growth of your business through perfectionism is feeling unable to delegate work to staff members. This can prevent you from spending valuable time working on your business, because you are always stuck in your business.

Being in business is hard, right? You've invested so much in growing your business that often the thought of handing it over to someone else can seem incomprehensible, I get it. However, it is possible to work with the clients you want to, build better relationships with your employees and free up more time to take your business to the next level. I know because I've worked with clients who have achieved it.

Value and worth: Often people will look to their competitors for the answers. Trying to model your business on what your competitors are doing, can sometimes cause you to miss the value you individually bring to the table. Understanding and applying your value requires self-awareness, understanding your strengths and the ability to leverage your mindset to grow and evolve your value as your business also evolves.

The good news is that it's possible to grow your mindset and develop innovative thinking tools that can span across all areas of your business. Mindset is an important part of being successful in business and in life and can be the "make it or break it" component to getting where you want to be.

CHAPTER 7

Develop and Manage Your Client's Trust

Trust is simple; don't lie or embellish or give cause for people to mistrust you. Always deliver what you promise and communicate, communicate, communicate. Trust is something that unequivocally must exist when you are involved in any relationship. Particularly, with their most significant investment of their life which is their property, whether buying or selling, people surrender their confidences to you and it should be handled with nothing but integrity.

Again, I've been very fortunate in my relationships over the years as they have all been forged on the foundation of trust. I am a person that says what I mean and mean what I say. I foster these relationships through trust and consistency. Nothing heads a deal south quicker than saying one thing and doing another; or shattering the fragile armour of trust.

At times, you will be confronted with situations that test your patience and faith, but I have trained myself to tackle this with positivity and keeping my eye on the big picture.

Here are examples of a situation that stands out from experience.

"Trust and Transparency"

I had a buyer contact me to view one of my own listings. The buyer agreed to work with me on this property and duly signed a buyer representation agreement. After several viewings of the home, the buyer was ready to come forward with an offer. I prepared the offer based on the buyer's request even though it was substantially under asking. My seller was not looking for a 'fire' sale (but my thinking was to get the ball rolling and start negotiations) while at the same time educating the buyer on the positives of the property, location and its features.

The seller reviewed the buyer's offer and as I expected, they signed back with a relatively high price, even though they had signed back substantially lower than asking price. After reviewing the sign back, the buyer felt that I had not worked in his best interest to have his offer price accepted.

We tried to convince the buyer of the value in the property and submit a revised sign back. The buyer refused and walked away from the property.

Several weeks later, I received another offer from a cooperating agent for this property, we spent about a week negotiating with the buyer. The paperwork went back and forth, finally having the offer accepted just under asking price. One of the conditions inserted in the offer was an assignment clause allowing the purchaser to potentially add another buyer's name for financing. All the conditions and clauses were accepted by seller and the deal was now firm.

Fast forward to a week before closing, I receive an amendment request adding another buyer's name to the contract. A light bulb went off when I saw the name. It turned out this was the same buyer that had put in the low ball offer several weeks earlier and was now working with another agent. They added the assignment clause knowing full well they were only going to qualify for full financing with both buyer's name on title.

As to be expected, my initial reaction was of disappointment and frustration. I was surprised the buyer would take this approach, considering his comments about what he felt this property was worth. He was adamant that the offer he put forth was as high as he wanted to go, stating he saw no additional value to the property. At the time, I was willing to work with him and take my time to show him other properties in the area to educate him on the market value and comparison. It appeared the buyer had realized the value in this property (perhaps after many weeks of potentially viewing other homes) and had come back to the idea of purchasing it.

From my experience, I have noticed sometimes people's pride and ego can get in the way and that can be difficult to work with. This buyer was fully aware he had signed a Representation Agreement with me for the purchase of this property. To bypass this, he initially placed the offer under his wife's name and added the assignment clause knowing full well he would be adding his own name closer to closing.

Ultimately, he ended up spending more to purchase the property. I knew I hadn't done anything wrong, so I contacted the agent and let them know what had happened. I have learned it is best to stand your ground, even if at times it may ruffle some feathers. This buyer had initially signed with me and I had presented an offer on behalf of him. He was in fact contracted to me for this property, therefore I was legally entitled to a portion of the commission the cooperating agent was collecting.

The cooperating agent's initial reaction was that of ignorance, implying he had no knowledge of this buyer's past offer. I produced the previous offer to substantiate my claims and involved my broker of record to clarify the real estate rules. This buyer's agent had no choice then to agree to share a portion of the commission.

This experience is a good example of standing by your convictions and knowing the rules. At the same time, learning to not dwell on such negative experiences and moving on is critical to your success. In the end, I had a happy seller and the home was sold.

A good businessperson needs to be able to put negatives behind them, because there will be plenty of times that trust will be broken and issues will arrive. Learning to not take anything personally will not only toughen up your skin, it will aid you across the board in doing well in Real Estate.

Building trust requires building or identifying an emotional connection between you and the client. Telling your clients what they need to hear versus what they want to hear, will ultimately build a better relationship. They will trust that you have their best interest at heart and are not just looking to earn their business, by being a 'yes man'!

You should know what motivates your client, such as children, location of choice, lifestyle, life change and the like. If you know that your client may be having issues in some of these or other areas, it's good to be able to provide an answer or refer another to help them solve their problems.

"Be open and honest"

I met with a prospective client who was looking to sell his house. From the outside the pictures of the property looked great! But upon entering the house, I could see that it needed A LOT of work. As he walked us from room to room, he was quick to point out what he had planned to fix. With every few steps he asserted "I'm going to fix this soon, don't worry about it!". But his words of reassurance did little to reassure me! It became glaringly obvious that the place needed more than what he thought it did.

There was a big mess in almost every room, and it seemed the further we walked through the house, the more fixing needed to be done. He continued to assure me that 'it will be fixed and not to worry about it'. Once we finished the walk through, he was curious what the house was worth (once the work would be completed of course). He had seen the potential of his house and not what it actually was – a tear down!

From my professional opinion, there really were only two options for his place: sell as is or tear it down completely! I knew I needed to be honest with him. Any work he thought he could do would take several months to complete. Even he acknowledged that perhaps he would need a contractor, asking if I could recommend one! There is always a risk in being honest with someone, not everyone wants to hear the truth. But I've learned there is no sense in not being honest and transparent with my clients. It is best to see the property as is than with rose colored glasses!

Being willing to help even though there may not be an immediate benefit to you, this will help build client confidence in you and your services. And as a result, they will be far more willing to listen to your advice in the future, thus leading to you helping them with a sale or purchase or enhancing your chances of them referring you and ideally the quality of your services.

Always respect your clients' time. In this day of general loss of courtesy and respect, especially when compared to the older generation, we should be mindful of what we ask a client for and what we take. Be aware of their time and schedules by doing the following to hold their respect at the top of your list.

- Return phone calls, as soon as possible.

- Immediately and thoroughly reply to emails.

- Don't be late for a scheduled call or a scheduled in-person meeting.

- Be mindful of promised call start and end times for calls. (If you ask for 10 minutes of their time, be sure to keep it to 10 minutes.) If it seems to be heading to more time, be mindful and inquire if the client can comfortably continue the conversation.

Be honorable with your commitments. This concept ties in with respecting peoples' time but goes a bit further. Consultants can't accomplish work without input (feedback, tangible assets, consent, etc.) from clients. You can't expect a client to do their part to uphold a timeline if you're not holding up your end of the agreement. This translates to the need to undertake the following:

- ☐ Keep appointments.

- Punctually get back in touch with any follow-up items promised.

- Frequently connect all progress made toward an agreed-to deadline (this is a great way of demonstrating you're always thinking of the client and it keeps the client up to speed in case others ask them about status).

Find Equal Ground. Sometimes people can articulate the problems they want to solve. Other times they just know the outcomes they want. Come closer to delivering on client expectations when you:

- Ask them to identify as closely as possible at the onset of working together what their goals ideally look like in the end.

- Communicate with complete transparency. We all have different expectations around information communications. Regardless of the industry we are in however, unless specifically noted, more is better. Group dispensation is a key component to a happy business transaction, which may mean:

- Writing deals, phone discussions, or in-person meetings when follow ups are required, send a group email to all parties involved.

- Maintain a central source of messages pertaining to that specific client and related files within shared files on work computers.

- Never assume information/requests sent were received. "I emailed her but didn't hear back" is a bad excuse for a 'pass the buck to the client' situation.

Be trustworthy: It's much easier, better and more satisfying to demonstrate your trustworthiness than to hide your deceptions. But I will assume since you're asking this question, you intend to act with integrity, and just want to know how to communicate that effectively to your clients.

Unfortunately, there are enough unprincipled agents that you'll often fight an uphill battle with new clients. There are some people that have heard bad stories about agents. There are some that have experienced it for themselves. And there are still others that will resent or distrust you no matter what, simply because they think you get paid too much for what you do. They'll identify themselves in the first conversation, so they're easy to spot. They've already decided to dislike you and already decided that you're a criminal and will watch you like a hawk for you to live up to these expectations and will likely manufacture wrongdoing if you don't provide them with it yourself.

So, you're dealing hopefully with a reasonable client and you are working hard in their best interest. Here are three tips to make sure they know you're looking out for them.

- An enormous part of sales is managing expectations. In the few cases where I've witnessed clients lose trust in me, it was expressed with the phrase *you never told me this could happen.* It wasn't that I'd lied to them, it wasn't that I'd acted unethically (which I pride myself on never doing), it was that something bad happened and they found it to be a surprise. Some common examples are things like your buyers lose the home because another offer is accepted. Or the home is under appraised, and the total costs are more than they anticipated, just to name a few. None of these are your fault or within your control. However, the better you prepare or manage your clients, the happier everyone will be. Here are some things I say to clients to help manage them:

- Buying and selling a home is stressful. It's natural to feel overwhelmed.

- It's impossible for us to know where the home will appraise. It's possible it could under-appraise, over-appraise, or come in at value.

- We can certainly negotiate as aggressively as you want. Just be aware that the risk you run is someone else making a higher offer at the same time. (I'm always surprised I must explain this to people but, I do.)

- In this market, you should be ready to lose a few homes before you finally get under contract on the one you'll buy, especially if it is a seller's market and the competition is rigid.

- And for the sellers, showing your home isn't fun and I will not sugar-coat it. There will be agents who don't show up for their scheduled appointments, agents who show without an appointment, or agents who are late, or early, or leave the lights on. We'll put notes around the house to try to manage this, but it always happens. The one thing you cannot control are the behaviours of others.

- Do what you say you're going to do. There is a lot of follow up involved with any clients, so pull the comps and send them like you said. Get that question answered about that ceiling stain. Find out why the last contract fell apart. When was the foundation repaired, again? This isn't so much about them trusting your integrity, it's about them trusting you not to drop the ball on something that will cost them money.

  The logic goes like this, *I had to ask three times for those comps*. What are they going to miss during the transaction? What if there's something they overlooked in the contract and our contract isn't valid? What if...

Keeping their trust requires very good note taking, self-discipline and time management.

- ☐ **Communication.** Stress is high when people are buying or selling a home. It disrupts their life, brings financial concerns to the surface, often provokes fights within families for varieties of reasons, and generally turns their world upside down. It adds to their stress by many degrees if they feel like they can't reach you for answers, and you don't respond in a timely fashion. Inevitably, you're inviting them to fuel all that stress into frustration with you. So be timely, be available and once again, answer your phone. To put some numbers on this, if you haven't answered their phone call twice in a row over the last couple days, you really should answer their next phone call. Any time you can't answer the phone, be sure you respond quickly with an email or text either answering the question or letting them know you're working on it. Don't let an email sit for more than 24 hours. If they emailed you late at night, you don't have to answer that night, but the next day before 12 is a good goal to set.

Do the unanticipated, this may be where you will truly add value to a relationship, and it goes a long way to create trust. An example of this would be if you have a client that has a child in school, look up the local schools in the area so they know you are working for and with them. It truly is a little thing, but people appreciate any thing that removes a bullet item on their checklist.

Authenticity is probably one of the biggest trust creators. We don't want to deal with people that we feel are dishonest, insincere or misleading. We look for friends and even colleagues that hold similar values to our own, authentic.

"It takes 20 years to build a reputation and five minutes to ruin it. If you think about that, you'll do things differently." — Warren Buffett

CHAPTER 8

Provide Worth

Understanding value and creating it is imperative for your client. If not, the 90-day window will pass, and they will move on to another real estate agent. Let them know you have their best interest at heart by making sure you have them in any advertising publications, in print and/or online. Keep your client's listing relevant online by periodically changing up the wording on the web page that you have going. Have an Open House and advertise it as much as you can and get some showings at the property. Ultimately, sell their home because they will be your greatest advocates for new business. And that is the best thank you that the client could provide, their trust and ensuing word-of-mouth marketing.

If it wasn't for my client base and their referrals, then I wouldn't have as much to be grateful for, so I make it a point to think about what I can do for them to show my gratitude. They are things that make sense for my clients and are of a practical and relevant nature. When my excellent clients move into their home, we prepare special welcome baskets, home-made to get them underway in their new homes. We will always follow this up with a call or a visit to their home as a part of a severely lacking personal touch that we don't find a lot in this industry or many industries, for that matter.

Here's the thing, at their essence, clients are always looking for value, just like you and I when we purchase something or use a service. Subsequently, when they see value, the chances of them making a commitment to work with you increase significantly. Value is not just about the sale, but for having a client and residual referrals from that client, for life. The idea is to make them feel that your service and ensuing value can't be duplicated, so they wouldn't consider going anywhere else. With value comes contentment, and with contentment comes true loyalty.

This may seem relatively easy and, in some situations, it is. However, in most cases, the main cost on bringing increased value to a client is a little bit more attention to detail as well as a larger outlay of time. We all know that there is a cost to our time, and we only have 24 hours in a day, but if your objective is adding value to your clients' experience, then you will find a way to make that a staple customer service practice.

"Try not to become a man of success, but rather try to become a man of value" – *Albert Einstein*

Check out these tips on ways you can add value to your way of thinking.

Be the specialist. When your client feels that you know your stuff, in other words you are a specialist in real estate, then your value rises inevitably. You must do things that make this come to life, be available, be educated on your client's area and do the market research. Being an authority gives your client a huge sense of security and this will lead to loyalty.

Understand your clients. Make a connection with your client, open them up to feeling understood. If you go about this in the right way, they will tell you everything, and then you will translate that into understanding. Once you understand, and they start to feel that you understand, because your actions imitate and bring into line with their feedback, your value is increased tremendously. It's a small thing that has a large impact in business.

Listen to your clients. Most brands and businesses just do not listen. Please, don't be that real estate professional that gets so involved in hearing their own voices that they turn potential clients away. I have had to discuss this with agents over time, and it gets down to listen twice as much as you speak. In your business life, if you listen more than you talk, then there is no doubt that you will be able to figure out how to create the most worth in what you are doing and easily be able to pass this along to your clients.

Wow your clients. Real estate is a very personal business, such that remembering things like birthdays, special occasions, etc., and thinking of them on those days absolutely increases value. We are all human and at the end of the day, if we feel that someone has done something special or out of the ordinary for us, then we feel beholden to the giver of such value. And with value comes a loyalty and that my friends, is the goal in this industry.

Look around at how many businesses of all shapes and sizes fail to do these small and basic things well, and they then wonder that when they ask their clients about brand value, the answers are all but silence. Value has always and will always be the businessperson's best friend. Figure out what it is that you can do for your consumer to ensure they value you so highly that they will be with you for life.

"You can make more friends in two months by becoming interested in other people than you can in two years by trying to get other people interested in you" – Dale Carnegie

CHAPTER 9

Be Successful with Your Best Dressed Self

You are responsible for your personal brand. Your professional relationships begin with a first impression. Doting over a business card is important, but more important is your personal brand, and that means you! It is in constant need of attention and polishing, as it is your personal business card in life. I can't impress upon you enough, the importance of personal presentation, personal hygiene and always putting your best foot forward, and attitude. This chapter will touch on everything from your appearance to the vehicle you drive. The old saying, dress to impress has not faded away. It is as relevant now as it was at any time. When wearing clothing that you look good in, your hair is well groomed and where applicable, your make up is perfect, you have no other option but to hit the ground running! This has many positive effects on you, and on how people will ultimately perceive you.

Let's start with pointing out how you feel when you are well dressed, looking sharp and ready to take on the day. You might have an important meeting today, maybe you are hoping to get that Million-Dollar listing, whatever the day holds for you, you look great and you feel respectable, right? As a result, you are likely going to be confident in yourself, confident in your abilities to do business, and you will likely be perceived the same way from your potential and/or current clients.

You will probably feel powerful, even smart. Your self-esteem is high, your self-worth is complimenting a feeling of influence that you are exuding because of being a sharp-dressed real estate professional. You are emitting an aptitude within your craft that says I will get this job done! And I will do it with class and confidence. Essentially your presence is felt, and you feel that effect in any social situation you find yourself in during the day.

Did you note everything mentioned above in the dress-for-success scenario was positive? Presence, self-worth, self-value, class, sharp, aptitude, confidence, and influence — they are all positive feelings, attributes and entailing consequences.

The above paragraph describes a much different state than the following paragraph. Set the scene, which is all too common. I'm sure you are aware of that awkward and uncomfortable feeling that happens when you put something on in the morning that doesn't fit quite well. It's either too big, too small or it's wrinkled, or some other imperfection exists like a thread hanging from a seam or cuff. Or you are running late for an appointment, you've run out of hair gel, or you've run out of mascara or whatever the uncomfortable condition. You know you are inevitably going to have a bad day, right?

It ends up being a full day of an awfulness, fussing with that wrinkled shirt as if it will iron itself, and pulling at a loose thread hoping your pant cuff doesn't let go. All the while, you're feeling self-conscious and overthinking that people are going to notice. Just how uncomfortable are you willing to end up spending your day?

Not being at your very best each day hardly seems worth giving up a perfectly productive day, doesn't it? Because it does affect what energy you are projecting to the world and what energy you are feeling inside.

What about how people look at you? How do people perceive you when you look well-dressed or how do you think they perceive you when you feel less than well-dressed? You may look good, but your lack of confidence in your attire shows in your demeanor and you will come off as lack-lustre. Studies have shown that wearing nice clothes in the office can affect the way people see you, how confident you're feeling, and even how you're able to think abstractly; not to mention how the perception will be held by the observer.

First impressions are inevitable. You can spend a lot of time trying to convince others of your great qualities, but you'll have a difficult time being perceived as genuine if your appearance doesn't sync with your values or your lifestyle as a real estate professional.

The image you elect to portray to others is a big resemblance of your true self, but the opposite effect can also be accomplished. Ever heard the saying "dress for success"? It still rings true. And guess what, you are being judged and you will be judged on your appearance, this is human nature, there is no getting away with it. That's just the reality of the world and you don't want to ever give anyone the opportunity to have negative judgements against you. Because you may not have control over much that exists outside of you, but you do have control over how the world sees you.

Here's a little scenario for you to ponder, you wake up in the morning and start the day with a delicious cup of coffee and hang out in your pajamas or maybe you stay in your sweats and the coffee is your only highlight in the morning. This conjures up a setting that is warm and fuzzy with a day that likely seems blurry with an overall ambition level that is safe to say, low. It's not the kind of day that takes you from zero to 100 in motivation and drive.

So now, change the circumstances up a bit and add a step to the scenario above. Take a few minutes and get dressed, I'll bet the results are incredibly different; it's as if you just drank another coffee. It's remarkable what a simple outfit can do for you when you button up that shirt or put something on that makes you feel ready for the day, your mindset shifts. The sky is suddenly brighter, and you can easily call up energy you didn't have before getting dressed. You've gone from slow to bring it on, in one small successful action; getting dressed.

Your clothing affects how you act and feel. Sneakers put you in the mood to exercise, and go for a walk. Heels enhance posture and change your frame of mind, and confidence takes over. Business attire will put you in the mindset to work, performing at your best. You've all the sudden changed your rapport with the world, you perceive yourself as more intelligent, you have clearer thought processes and you are all of the sudden feeling like the professional person that you are.

In real estate, there really are no dress codes, except for your own sense of right and wrong. My rule has always been that I dress a little better than I expect my audience (clients) to be dressed. If I am going to be attending a function where there are lots of opportunities for networking, then I will always dress to impress. Otherwise, I find that I might miss opportunities that I would have been able to seize because I felt uncomfortable or less than confident with my attire.

These days, clothing manufacturers are creating clothing lines that enhance your appearance but are also very comfortable to wear because it's an important part of life, both function and form. Back in the day, businesspeople who travelled were very concerned with how they would iron their clothes after a flight or how they would have their clothes pressed for their meetings after a long drive. Clothing has come a long way; pressing, steaming and water wicking are not much of a concern anymore, thanks to our innovative clothing manufacturers.

Because your appearance is also influential to others, not just yourself, it's important to present a professional image to coworkers and clients. Being in the workplace often entails meeting new people, interacting with coworkers, and communicating with managers.

Give your best impression in every way possible, so that no one can hold unjust biases against you because of how you present yourself. Let nothing stand in the way of your road to success.

You should never compare yourself to another in this area of your life. Everyone has different standards when it comes to overall physical presentation. If you are dressed to your best and you are feeling sharp and confident in how you are presenting, then that is all that matters.

Now, let's take your appearance one step further, so we can now talk about personal hygiene. By this I mean how your hair is done and how your make-up is applied, the scent you may be wearing. If you are a female, this speaks to what image it is you want to depict. If you are a younger woman, then wearing make-up is likely an essential part of starting your day. Not too much, not too little. You never want to look like you've just gotten out of bed or that you are sickly if you are pale skinned.

My daughter used to say that's how she looked when she wasn't wearing make-up, especially if she wasn't wearing mascara or a wee bit of cover-up under her eyes.

It really is different for each woman but according to my daughter, it helps you feel put together and ready to get on with the day. Conversely, you don't want to look like you're off to the club! It's about a tasteful balance in your presentation. Again, you don't want to make your clients or anyone you meet throughout your day feel uncomfortable. If you're overdoing your eye shadow or the eyeliner, you could put off the person you're in a meeting with. It then becomes a distraction. Keep it simple and tasteful and don't give anyone the opportunity to judge or misjudge you.

Then there is the hair discussion, and this obviously applies to both men and women. Here too you must put your best "head" forward.

Keep yourself well groomed, keep on top of root growth and hair products. We all have a style that fits our personalities, keep on top of it as you would your clothing.

It is all part of your personal greeting card and again, you will feel smarter, sharper and more professional, if you give yourself no reason to feel like you are not at your very best.

You may want to consider doing some of these things to keep you on top of your hygiene game. Keep accessories and products you may need to promote a fresh feel and look in your vehicle, as I and many of my colleagues do. The kind of toiletries that are great to travel with are items like deodorants, hair gel and gum for fresh breath. Other things I've heard people travel with are hairbrushes, for obvious reasons and lint brushes especially if they are pet owners or they are going to a home with pets. I have talked with people who have allergies to pets, so they often travel with antihistamines and keeping Advil for headaches on board is also a good practice.

Some other good gear to consider are, spare shoes and boots, depending on the time of year, an extra blazer or sweaters in case of the dreaded spillage of coffee or food. So, the moral of this story is to be prepared for just about any scenario. Better to have too many options available to you than not enough, especially when you need something and it's right there at your disposal. You'll be smitten with yourself for having everything you need, particularly when you need it.

How does this advice fit into your everyday style? In today's casual office dress code, dressing up can have a big effect on not only how you look but also how others treat and respect you. There is no downside to being well dressed from the top of your head to the tip of your toes, you are more confident, you are seen as more intelligent, and you are regarded well by others in your profession as well as regarded well by potential clients. What is the downside? There is none!

The bottom line is that your physical presentation is like your business card in life. You will make it easy for yourself to be successful and professional if you are dressing from head to toe for success.

What you wear affects you, and it affects others, and can influence your company's reputation. With the proper goal in mind of aiming towards excellent productivity, a well-dressed individual can improve work ethic, and consequently achieve maximum results.

Poorly dressed workers will often defer to suited ones, and suited professionals sense a heightened respect, backing down less than they might have otherwise.

In study, participants who dressed up were more likely to engage in abstract, big picture thinking like a CEO, while those less well-dressed concerned themselves with minor details.

"Like it or not, how we each present ourselves to the world, by way of our appearance, attire, behavior, and speech, all send messages on our behalf"
— Susan C. Young

CHAPTER 10

How Does Your Vehicle Present?

I would be remiss not to touch on another, maybe not so obvious aspect of personal presentation, and that's your vehicles' presentation. This is an absolute extension of who we are and how we show the world that we are successful. This is something that we can only make the best of most times, until we get some positive financial remuneration coming in through the door. There is an old saying that a clean car runs better. I always feel my car runs better clean, I feel better driving it and when it's clean, it makes me feel clean. Weird to some, but to others, this is perfectly relatable.

However, you may have a car that isn't exactly what you would like it to be, or it doesn't reflect where you see yourself positively in life and that's okay. The best thing to do is to work with what you have because until you are driving the car you want to be driving, it doesn't cost much to keep the one you are driving clean and presentable. Something to bear in mind is that there will be times, maybe 20% to

30% of the time you may have clients in your car. And trust me when I say that it will be the time that your car isn't up to your standards that you will get a request to have someone travel with you. There are some people that are pleased to drive with their real estate professionals, rather than go on their own to particular properties. And you may find this in conditions if they are going to more rural properties.

The benefit for some clients may be that they would like to spend time in the same vehicle with their agent to discuss real estate matters; it's a captive audience. They also may want to spend time picking your brain, this is often the case. Ultimately, this drive-along scenario can be advantageous because you are building a relationship and that is always the end goal.

Let's go over a few steps to help you get and maintain a clean and well-presented car — starting from the outside to the inside. There is some advice to get the best out of what you have so you are not feeling badly about your mode of transportation, until which time that you can invest in a car that you want to be driving.

Car wash: To get your vehicle's body looking good is to give it a thorough cleaning with car-wash soap and water. Once it's completely dry, look over the paint surface and evaluate any damage you see. And take note of any stone chips, dings, scratches and dents on the metal.

Paint chips and scratches: These are easy and relatively inexpensive fixes that you can handle on your own. You can touch up small scratches and chips with touch-up paint, available at your car dealership and at some auto-parts stores. Make sure you get an exact color match. Touch-up paint usually comes in a small bottle with an applicator brush in the lid. Or use a small, pointed artist's brush and cover the scratch by going over it in tiny spots. Let this paint dry for at least a day or two before polishing the car.

To remove or minimize the many fine surface scratches most cars accumulate, you can have the car professionally buffed at a body shop or car wash. This buffing will take out minor scratches and greatly improve the car's overall appearance.

Most cars made in the past 8 to 10 years have a "clear coat" paint finish. That means a thin color layer is coated with a thicker layer of a clear, lacquer-like coating. Whether you are polishing with a buffer or by hand, make sure the polish you use is safe for clear coat finishes if that's what's on the car.

Dents: As for dents, minor dents and dings in body panels can be very unappealing but getting them fixed at a body shop can be costly. One viable alternative is called paintless dent removal. This method uses special tools to massage out small dents from the inside.

Inside appearances of your car are equally as important as the outside. Considering how much time we spend in our cars, it's hardly surprising they suffer from smells, spillages and frequently much worse (for anyone with children) all kinds of odd food crumbs and smears. These then form bacteria, which start to smell, and before you know it, your car is more like a wastebasket than the second most valuable thing you own.

Follow these simple tips to prevent germs building up and restore a car's interior to its sales area splendour.

Clutter: First thing to do is clear out the clutter, get rid of that festering sandwich crust and crumbs from inside the door pocket along with the rotting banana skin from under the front seat and any other rubbish that is hidden in the bowels of your vehicle.

Car mats: Clean up your car mats, it's a difficult life being a car mat. Because they're designed to be trampled all over, so a bit of soap and water wouldn't hurt. Spray on an interior cleaner, wash it off with a hose or in your laundry tub, then hang them out and they could well be dry by the time you've finished doing the rest of the car.

Ventilation: Clean your car's ventilation system, first thing to do is close off all the air vents. Turn the ignition on, turn the heater blower up to full speed and open the vents, one at a time. This will blast dust out of the system. Once done, give it 10 minutes for everything to settle then start vacuuming up the dirt that's been dislodged. Use the brush attachment for the seats and carpets and remember to slide the front seats backward and forward so you can get right under them.

Dusting: Now you can start dusting. Use a soft cloth for dusting the inside. This has the double benefit of not scratching glossy materials but it's good at trapping the dust.

Leather and fabric seats: Now it's time to clean the seats. If they're leather, use a leather cleaner. If the seats are fabric, use a fabric cleaner. The seats will be left a little damp so leave the windows open until everything is dry.

Windows: To finish off, use a car glass cleaning product for windows. Work left to right on one side of the window; top to bottom on the other. Then if a smear is left behind, you'll be able to tell which side it's on.

Once you've got your car clean and fresh, the trick is to keep up on it. The reason that's so important is that you don't want a client to surprise you with a mutual travel day and you are doing a little freak inside because you were caught off guard.

And you should feel pretty darn good about yourself once you've got your vehicle up to its magnificent perfection.

"The cleanliness of your car is a good thumb-rule for your overall organization"
— Anonymous

CHAPTER 11

Stay in Touch

Without keeping conversations going, there are no chances for keeping in touch and the last thing you want to do is only reach out to people when it serves you. You won't gain too many loyal followers that way. And it will have a trickle-down effect on your business outcomes. When you stay in touch, this means you are also visible in your community, which is where you want to be observable.

I will often attend local functions and community events that keep me evident and relevant. Every time my town or close-by towns have events, whether for adults or children, I am there, I am talking to everyone and anyone I can to make sure that I am visible and remembered. However, I do realize that this can be a real challenging part of this business, but it is necessary for overall success. And I also find it unfortunate that we place negative correlations around reaching out to people. We should keep in touch because we truly enjoy it and we genuinely want to know what's going on in someone's life.

I came across an interesting word that appropriately addresses the complications that are relevant with staying in touch. *Sonders*. If you Google the definition, it means: *"It's the realization that each random passerby is living a life as vivid and complex as your own – populated with their own ambitions, friends, routines, worries and inherited craziness. It's an epic story that continues invisibly around you like an anthill sprawling deep underground, with elaborate passageways to thousands of other lives that you'll never know existed."*

Once we put what happens to the entire world into perspective, we can look at some good tips on how you can do your best to make sure you are staying in touch whenever and wherever we can.

- Start at the beginning by going through your most valuable commodity, your client database. This can be an arduous task and looking at it can be daunting, but it's essential. And let's face it; your network will determine your net worth. Handle this task with all the care you can and organize your lists into longer and shorter-term clients.

- Let grudges go from your past and pick up the phone, re-connect. This is one of the biggest issues that people have that hold them back in business. Look at it this way, we are moving forward, leave the past in the rear-view because that's not the direction we are travelling. Take the higher road, you never know what could be waiting for you.

- Try to position yourself as the expert in all things real estate, whether it's big or small. You should try and add an informative module to your communications when talking or emailing your client base. You want to set yourself up as the person, people go to for any information. You definitely want your network to think of you inevitably when your advice is needed. There should be a comfort level that people feel when they have questions and they want to call you; which would also imply that you should answer your phone, it's an obvious statement but it needs to be said.

- Keeping in touch with your network means setting up reoccurring lunches, coffees, phone call checkpoints or monthly meetings. Build this frame of mind naturally into your week-to-week calendar so that you're continuously making notes on who to connect with and to always be cycling back into your database. It should feel organic and never dreaded.

In the business world, an often-quoted statistic is that it costs six to seven times more to obtain a new client than to retain an existing one. The same applies to real estate. Previous clients are low-hanging fruit when it comes to real estate. Unlike potential clients who read your blogs, see your profiles and reviews online or click through to your website, past clients have worked directly with you. They know you and they know how you work, and if you've done a good job for them, they have a positive impression of you and give you a great review. You don't have to spend a lot of time or money to get their business again or to get a positive referral.

As a part of a yearly business plan, every agent should have goals for staying in touch with past clients. It should never be a one-off strategy, or a one-time event, action or approach and it should not be reactive rather than proactive. The best agents dependably cultivate the relationships they have with former clients. These agents likely use a calendar to track their past clients' notable anniversaries and see the efforts or actions required as just another part of their marketing plan.

Though the golden rule here is that you should only be in touch if you have something of value to offer. Just showing your face, posting about how great you are or throwing your clients on an email spam list won't do it. If you are irritating, assertive or reach out only for the sake of reaching out, this plan will surely fail. Make contact for a good reason, such as offering valuable market insights.

The best real estate agents are subtle and considerate about the ways they approach their past clients to produce referrals. Here are some imaginative ways to do just that.

- ☐ ***Use real estate referrals to get in touch.*** Receiving referrals from past clients is what every agent endeavours to accomplish, not only is it possible business in the form of a qualified lead, but it is also a chance to contact a past client. Double bonus. Upon receiving a referral from a former client, you should immediately call that client, or send either a handwritten or electronic message. This is a built-in strategy for staying in touch and thanking them for the referral.

  The client will be appreciative that you recognized their referral. Second, it's a chance to engage with a past client, and you should always take the opportunity to do that. What this allows you to do is, update them about the market; ask about their home, their family or their job. Ask some open-ended questions about their situation and identify occasions to stay in touch. And be sure to put the next reach-out onto your calendar.

  If they ask about the home for sale down the block or tell you about a home they drove by in the neighborhood, use it as an excuse to follow up with the sale price or information about the home. They may mention an upcoming kitchen or bath renovation. Provide them with a referral to your preferred contractor or designer. If you find out one of their kids is graduating high school or achieved some success, follow up with a small gift, it's nice to be thought of from the clients' perspective and people remember the little things.

Finally, when the referral buys or sells using you, send a gift to the referring client and follow up with a second thank-you. Again, it's not surprising but it's the right thing to do, hence, appropriate. The key point to take away from this is that a referral immediately provides an opportunity for you to be in touch with a former client.

- ☐ **Provide a mini CMA:** These days, there are so many ways for homeowners and past clients to get a feel for their home's value. Access to online listings is ubiquitous, information is readily available to them, from every direction. But not all homeowners are in the know, or care to take the time to know the comparable or to better understand the market. That is, they won't make the effort themselves. That's not to say they wouldn't like to know what their home is worth; they would. And that's where a good real estate agent comes in.

As part of your marketing plan, send a mini CMA to your clients once a year, or maybe twice a year depending on the real estate market. Put it on your calendar and spend a few hours or a few days putting each mini market analysis together. It's a way to be in touch with clients one-on-one and provide valuable information. You must be certain the mini CMA does not come across like you want your client to sell or are looking for a listing. Be clear about your intentions: that you are simply staying in touch and that you thought they might like to know what's going on in the neighborhood and how their home would fare.

Mini CMAs can be done electronically, so that your former clients can see the photos and listing information. It's a gesture that most clients will appreciate.

- ☐ **Just listed and sold cards:** Typically, real estate agents get a new listing and pull an area for a radius search in and around their new listing. Their objective? To show their faces and advertise themselves to possible sellers and to get the information out about their new listings to all the neighbors. This makes sense, and reliable mail marketing to an area has proven successful for thousands of agents over time. It's the consistency of the mailing to these neighbours that keeps an agent front and center of future clients while showcasing their expertise and experience in the neighborhood. You can send those same cards to past clients, even if they live in a different neighborhood or town. Your past clients want to know that you are successful, that they chose a winner. If they liked you and they had a pleasant transaction, they will be happy to see your accomplishments and maybe even go the extra step to keep you in mind for referrals.

There is no better way to show you are busy and active in the market than by sending out cards for every home you sell and every home you list. They are common and expected by consumers everywhere. They take little to no effort to glance at, look at it in detail or even toss. For every home you list for sale, have a list for past clients and make this an automated process.

- ☐ **Newsletters:** The email newsletter business is thriving and for good reason. It's a very easy, low-impact way to be in touch with clients. An email newsletter is just another creative way of having past clients see you and keep you top of mind. There are two very important thoughts when deciding to employ a regular newsletter. One is how often you send them out, and the other is the content you should use to be relevant. The minimum frequency should be once per quarter and the maximum would be every six weeks; this one is the sweet spot so as not to overbear the recipients and also not letting too much time go by. Bear in mind that the content of the newsletter really matters. Provide excellent content on a regular basis, your clients will be excited to open your newsletter and even look forward to it.

What's great about newsletters is that they can be easily forwarded. Imagine your past client has a coffee date with a friend who remarks that they are looking to buy a home in the near future. You want to be sure that you are top of mind with this past client, both because you've done an excellent job getting them their new home, but also because they may have received an email two days earlier or a few days later, hence, keeping you at the top of their mind. You better believe they will forward it to their friend with some positive words about you, and that my friend, is the best marketing you can receive in real estate.

Every real estate agent should employ a process for setting up a regularly scheduled email newsletter. Set the system and framework of the newsletter once and then simply go in each time and add four or five articles or updates. Try your best to make sure the content adds value to the reader and is only local informative. People like data and stats, particularly when it pertains to them or their area. And if they learn something or get ideas from your newsletter, they are more likely to keep opening up your newsletters and reading them in the future. The more they read them, the more likely they are to think of you as the local real estate expert, which is a handle that you want.

- ***Drop off gifts — In Person:*** For years, agents have sent cards and cute gifts to clients to mark a birthday or the anniversary of their home purchase, in addition to holiday cards. But in the days of email, smartphones and the internet, as a society, we've stepped away from the personal interactions. It shouldn't be that way, and this is now the out-of-the-box thinking that used to be commonplace, things have come full circle.

Knocking on the door of a former client on a late afternoon or early evening is your best shot of getting someone who is actually at home. As a familiar face and with gift in hand, you have a great chance of being well received. While some people might be taken aback, others will appreciate the gesture, and the gift and give you a few minutes of their time to touch base, catch up and stay relevant.

An inexpensive gift for clients on Valentine's Day might be some attractively packaged homemade cookies. Such a gift would be unexpected and will surely help you stand out. This strategy may not work across the board for all clients and you know them best. Choose wisely and know that this may only be an option for a fraction of your past real estate clients. Otherwise, showing up unannounced in today's culture could even backfire.

- ***Learn what works and what doesn't:*** Whatever you do to stay in touch with former clients, there's always the chance you may rub someone the wrong way. Be prepared to back off if you sense that you have irritated someone. Take them off your list (especially if they request it) and be certain you don't reach out to them in that way in the future. Though it may feel frustrating, or you might be inclined to take it personally, don't. Some people simply don't like snail mail, email or any sort of non-essential communication.

Also, don't forget that many of your previous clients, no matter how great they were to work with, simply go back to their lives. Absent the real estate business, they may not appreciate the contact or are too busy to stay in touch. It doesn't mean they don't like you. But there will always be those who don't want to be "bothered" by you. In that case, focus your energies on clients who are a good source of referrals.

The key to success in real estate is a consistent and growing book of business and a frequent flow of referrals from your former clients. It's so important for any agent to identify strategies that work for this growth and employ them consistently. For the referrals to come, not only do you have to give great service, be honest and provide a quality experience, but you must constantly *touch* your past clients both online and offline. The more they see you, the more they will think of you and the better chance you have of receiving a referral.

And remember, always provide quality communications. Don't spam clients or call asking for referrals. The best real estate agents provide value added service and engage clients with something to offer. Before you reach out to a client in any form of communication, ask yourself this important question, "Would I find this interaction helpful?" If not, don't do it because it will defeat the whole purpose of this exercise.

I found this interesting and appropriate quote from *Mahatma Gandhi*, he spoke of being blinded by the hunt for success and losing sight of who you are.

A customer is the most important visitor on our premises. He is not dependent on us. We are dependent on him. He is not an interruption in our work. He is the purpose of it. He is not an outsider in our business. He is part of it. We are not doing him a favor by serving him. He is doing us a favor by giving us an opportunity to do so. – Mahatma Gandhi

CHAPTER 12

Work-Life Balance

This is all the discussion of the last decade or maybe even more than the last decade — the ever-prevalent work-life balance. Incidentally, more companies are making it a common part of their day-to-day conversations in the workplace. Given that in this work climate of our contemporary times, we are all so connected, there isn't a clear division between work and personal life anymore and because of this, the average person's burn-out rate is enormously high.

The thing to keep in mind throughout this chapter is that there is actually *no* perfect formula for work-life balance. It doesn't look the same for everyone. It's not the perfect visual you may conjure in your mind's eye of making a living and yoga in the park. You wake up early, go for a run, have breakfast already to go, shower, and off to the office you head, happy, healthy scenario, right? The idea here is that although there is no perfect balance, there are realistic ones. Figuring out your own personal balance is a process that happens over time, not in one day. And some days, you'll have more work than time for things like hobbies and some days, the reverse will be true.

More and more organizations are implementing best practices when it comes to achieving work-life balance for their employees. This is because they know that doing so will be beneficial not only to their staff but also to their company productivity and revenue as well. In fact, it remains to be one of the more important assets in the workplace, even surpassing compensation. Some of the areas that we need to consider in the best practices are easy to bring to the forefront of your mind, yet hard to do, especially where real estate professionals are concerned.

Your livelihood depends on you answering your phones and being available for your clients, morning, noon and night. And this is a particular challenge with the higher maintenance clients. We all have them, we all know them, and that's what we do because that's how we make a living. But this is also why we have such a high burn-out rate or expiry date as it has been referred to by many. But the kindest thing you can do for yourself is to keep your health in check. Consequently, you have to self-care and manage this on your own in this industry.

You should consider putting some safeguards in place to not only protect yourself but to also protect your family and in some cases your marriage. It's like anything, you are only as strong as your weakest link. And if your home life is suffering because of work, it becomes a slippery slope. When things aren't healthy at home, it spills over into your work life and vice versa.

Below are some examples of what you can consider and implement in terms of best practices to encourage a good work-life balance for their employees. You can take some of these suggestions and integrate them into your own work-life on some levels.

Try flexible working hours. Some employers allow their employees to work from home for a day a week or every other week, so they can attend to important personal matters even while working. In real estate perhaps, you consider making sure that you have one day to attend to your own personal appointments or personal calls to better contribute to your own family during the traditional 9 to 5 hours, making sure that family and work are contributed to equally.

Try alternative working days. Some of the most effective alternative work schedules allow letting employees work 10 hours a day and have three days of rest. This can also translate into real estate, so you take a day off occasionally. You know that your workday is already more than eight hours, more like 10 to 12 if not more in a day. Allow yourself an indulgent day here and there, you deserve it and it's okay and it's healthy for business and family!

Autonomy and personal growth. If the members of an organization can choose their schedules and the days within a week when they will report for work, they will be given the autonomy to make decisions regarding their work and personal life. This is beneficial to employees because they become more confident about themselves and more assertive. Also, this will boost employee morale, making them happy and content employees.

As a real estate professional, this is also something you can consider because you are taking care of both state and church, so to speak. We all just think and feel better if we are not tied to a schedule that can interfere in our ability to manage our life in all aspects.

Increase your focus. A workplace with life and works best practices is important to ensure employees will be more concentrated at work. By giving employees the chance to report and do their jobs during hours when their mind is working and their focus is at its peak, you will enhance their productivity and more work can be completed, as they need not worry about meeting commitments on family and work. This work-life balance scenario is a good one. We really do have a hard time keeping focus when in the back of our mind we are concerned with issues like doctor or dentist appointments, children's sports schedules, aging parents, whatever the situation is, it just works better. You will definitely be better engaged in the task at hand when you allow yourself certain freedoms.

Your personal well-being. Flexible work weeks and work hours give employees time to rest and reduce stress. Instead of spending hours simply to get to and from work, employees can use this time to start work and finish early in the comforts of their homes even for one day in a week. This can also lessen the stress at work and give them more time to rest or exercise, so they can be ready for another challenging work week. Less stress can reduce the risks for medical conditions and allows individuals to have healthier lives. If employees can manage their work schedule, work and life will be less stressful for them. Again, cut yourself a break and take the above advice and be healthier in your mind and in your body because you are important.

Improve your productivity. By letting employees enjoy flexible work schedules, employers ensure that their employees will be working when they are most productive. Say, an employee is not a morning person. If an employee is permitted to report to work at a later hour and stay after office hours, this employee will be able to concentrate more with the tasks at hand. There are night owls and find it hard to focus in the mornings. Letting them perform their duties during hours that conform to their biological clocks will make them more efficient and productive with productivity reaching up to 21 percent.

You too, may be more productive and therefore more successful. A lot of our clients have off-time schedules as they work through the day, so we are working evenings or on weekends. So, through the day, from time to time, let the phone go to voicemail (but be sure to check and return the call), start a little later in the day and go for a massage.

Every day there is something to do, but not every day has to be frenzied. Some of the stress of the job is self-inflicted. For example, failing to file documents or to respond to emails will leave you swamped by the end of the week. And that can easily turn into the end of the following week and on and on. Now that's for sure going to lead to a frenzied and overwhelming feeling. Further to the above suggestions, think about the fact that there are things you can do to manage your work-life better.

Stay on top of daily tasks. Make life simpler and more efficient by simply staying on top of your easy daily tasks. For instance, schedule a specific block of time, say an hour, to go through and respond to emails at the same time every day. And schedule time to do the following:

- Scanning, emailing and filing documents
- Answer your voicemails
- Daily Cultivation of Leads (i.e., blogging, sending newsletters, updating e-mail database, etc.)
- Update your calendar

If you do these small tasks each day, you will save yourself a lot of time in the long run. Make a list of your 15-minute tasks and block out the first two hours of your day, the last two hours of your day, or one hour at the beginning and end of your day to complete these tasks. My point here is that you need to do these things regardless of how you make the time, just make the time. Your life will be better and more organized for it.

Manage your time. Time management is split in real estate, you have personal time and work-life time parameters. As your own boss and with the type "A" personality of most of the real estate agents I know, taking time off can be an afterthought when you are focused on building your business.

However, without taking appropriate time for your personal life and self-care, you will end up burned out and your business will inevitably suffer. You must learn to set aside personal time without concessions. If your kid's hockey games land on Fridays in the fall, and it's not negotiable for you to attend, let your clients know your schedule up front, it's called managing expectations.

Managing your time also involves fitting things comfortably into your schedule. There are going to be times when your workload is overwhelming, it is just the nature of the business. But you can manage those times much easier if you learn early how to space out your schedule so that you don't overload your days:

- Give yourself time to get to and from appointments without feeling rushed.
- Try to avoid scheduling back-to-back meetings.
- Allow wiggle room in your schedule; don't book every block of your day.
- Put your personal time on your work schedule as a fixed appointment.

Put boundaries on your time. You have to set up boundaries for your work hours. While it is true that the best agents give their clients 24/7 devotion, the fact is no one has 24 hours out of any day to give.

Make sure that your office hours are well communicated directly and, on your website, and business cards. For your actual clients and close partners, give out your personal 24/7 number.

Make it something exclusive and valuable that you offer certain clients. That way, you can offer responsive service to all of your clients but your select clients know that you will go above and beyond for them.

Don't be afraid to ask for help. Strong people and hard workers often have a hard time asking for help. The problem with that is that you end up wasting a lot of time and making life mostly harder by trying to do it all on your own.

Keep realistic expectations. Again, many new agents enter the business thinking that they will start pulling in six figures a year while barely working, I'm here to tell you that nothing could be further from the truth. When figuring out a good work-life balance as a real estate agent, you have to set realistic expectations.

Knowing that until you have time to make a few sales and a healthy pipeline of new leads, your days will be consumed with work and knowing this will create a happier work-life balance. The goal is to make the work that you do immensely productive, ultimately you want to work smarter, not harder. There is a goal for you to work towards!

One way to accomplish this is to give yourself a regular day or two off each week. Choose one or two of your typically lightest days and make at least one a part-time day and the other a day off. Turn your phone off and shut down your computer to resist doing work on those days.

When it comes to building up your real estate business, your goal should be to maximize your time so that you can provide extraordinary service to all of your clients. Why not procure some help for that?

If you are the type who relishes your independence as a one-man or woman operation, you can hire an administrative assistant. Virtual assistants can take over many daily tasks that eat into your daily schedule including:

- Updating and Uploading Your Listings
- Making Small Changes to Your Website
- Managing Your Contact Databases
- Handling Filing and Data Entry
- Submitting Paperwork
- Creating Reports and Presentations
- And More

If your business is booming and you need more in-depth help, how about expanding into a partnership? Is there someone that you know in the business working as an independent agent who would add to your business? Maybe it's time to invite them out for lunch to discuss a partnership.

The bottom line in the struggle for work-life balance is that you matter and your personal life matters. We need to be aware of how we care about ourselves which has a big effect on business and your personal relationships.

CHAPTER 13

Be Authentic

This is when you are representing your true self and your true beliefs. And you know it, when you meet someone who is living an exceptionally constructed and authentic life, it's like a breath of fresh air. These people are rare, and it takes courage and self-confidence to be who you really are, despite reactions from skeptics and their efforts to bring you back to conformity.

We often find ourselves judging a person's authenticity by the passion and commitment they have. Unquestionably, part of being authentic is standing up for what you believe in and speaking your truth, even if it is not what others want to hear. We will ask, what are they authentic to?

People can be dedicated to and enthusiastic about a lot of things, but this by itself is not enough. Authenticity is more than when someone believes in what they say or acts in a way that is consistent with their beliefs.

An inauthentic person is equally able to stand up and say what they truly believe. We ought not to judge authenticity purely by the passion a person has for what they say. The more important part of the authenticity question is to look at the character of the person. What's behind what they say?

Authentic people possess several common characteristics that show they are psychologically mature and fully functioning as human beings. Take a read of the below and see how close to authentic you are. There are grey areas with people, particularly if you are dealing with clients and prospective clients and some tact may be needed. You will see what I mean once you start going through these points. But let's face it, nothing more inspirational than being around an authentic person; or even better, being that authentic person.

They are harmless but honest, the problem is some people can't take honesty and are way too sensitive.

- ☐ They aren't afraid to express their own opinions even though those sentiments might not reflect that of the masses. They have accurate perceptions of reality.

- ☐ They are motivated to action by an internal compass rather than something outside of themselves.

- ☐ They're proud of their unique characteristics that make them stand out from the crowd. And they understand their own motivations.

- ☐ They have exceptional regular rituals, for example starting the day off with a chapter of a good book or preparing for the next day, a day beforehand, with purpose.

- ☐ Conversations with authentic people are typically grounded in depth and wisdom rather than gossip or mindless chatter.

- ☐ They enjoy their own company; they do not need to fill quiet time with noise or people for the sake of filling time.

- ☐ Experiences are more valuable than things and stuff for the authentic individual.

- ☐ They make the most out of the circumstances they find themselves in, be the situation good, bad or indifferent.

- ☐ Talking less is key for them because they will typically reserve their opinions until they are fully informed and can add value to a discussion.

- ☐ Listening closely is an apparent characteristic because they're captivated with exploring the depths of others, this is how they form relationships.

- ☐ They don't often complain, and they take full responsibility of their own existence.

- ☐ They can express their emotions freely and clearly.

- ☐ Self-esteem and confidence will always appear when you meet these people because they have nothing to hide. However, they are open to learning from their own mistakes.

- ☐ It's not upsetting to them when someone clearly dislikes them. The good opinion of others is not their concern.

- ☐ They see beauty and perfection in things that other people just miss.

- ☐ They never apply advice given without initially reading the leader that lives inside of themselves.

- ☐ Support for others and an authentic desire to see people grow and reveal their full potential is a goal for them.

- ☐ They let go of critical and negative people, whether in work or in personal life, and will not typically harbour ill-will or bad feelings against those people. They accept themselves and other people.

- ☐ Unification is all they see when they look out at the world, in all its intricacies.

Conversely, inauthentic people possess the below characteristics. These are easily distinguishable from the list above.

- Are self-deceptive and unrealistic in their perceptions of reality.

- Look to others for approval and to feel valued.

- Are judgemental of people.

- Do not think things through clearly.

- They tend to have a bit of a hostile personality.

- They have difficulty expressing their feelings easily and clearly.

- Are not as open to learning from their mistakes, they make excuses rather than take responsibility.

- Do not understand their own impetuses, they tend to act emotionally rather than rationally.

A good thing to note is, if behind what a person says and does is distrustful and self-deceptive, then no amount of passion will give them an authentic edge.

When authenticity prevails, we see clear and without judgement. Authenticity is ultimately about those qualities that show healthy non-defensive attributes and psychological maturity. Those are the qualities we need to look for in ourselves and others.

One thing to remember is that people will not like you, if they don't know who you are. Your work can be exemplary but if there isn't a connection through authenticity, then you won't develop a lot of followers. People may not even know why they can't connect with you, but most of us have an innate instinct when it comes to authenticity.

It is of highest importance that the way you feel inside, your values and beliefs of who you are, and all things being equal, then they should match what the outside you emulate. If the two are disjointed, that's when people's radars tend to go up, and they feel there's something about you that isn't truthful, hence a detection of inauthenticity.

Some examples of inauthentic behaviours are people who hide their true selves because they fear the truth will be damaging to, in this case, their careers. For example, a working mother may be less apt to say that she can't make a 5pm meeting because the reality is, she must pick up her children from daycare. She may view it as a deterrent to being promoted because she thinks she is seen as unreliable in the workplace. In the same way, an obligation that someone may have to take care of their aging parents interferes in the ability to show up and be 100% present at work every day. We cover these things up, so we don't look inadequate or like we have a life outside of work, rather than be honest about our life trials. We hide so many things that it becomes hard to remember what and who we are and why we do what we do.

The problem is that this choice to be dishonest makes the workplace or the industry worse for everyone, because it contributes to an environment where no one feels entitled to be human. When people uncover themselves by choice, they feel more open, and the workplace becomes more inclusive.

This is not to say we must open our lives up to everyone we meet, but there is some level of truth that we should easily divulge so people know we are human, because guess what? We *are* human. And with humanity comes adversity and with adversity comes the opportunity for authenticity. This being open and authentic should not be confused with making excuses for not getting things done, but an opportunity to make yourself more relatable to others in life, hence living a more authentic life.

Clients who feel they can identify with you are more likely to do business with you. On the most fundamental level, people do business with people they like. If you're trying to shield certain aspects of who you are, people will feel like there's some invisible shroud surrounding you.

Lifting that veil gives you the chance to relate with clients and even coworkers with a deeper connection. If we are who we are, then people will either like us, or they won't. But it won't be because of something we're doing or not doing. People sometimes don't gel, and for no reason, just personality conflicts or differences in presentation skills or the like, and that's okay if it's not because of being less than we can be authentically.

If we spend our days in black suits and ties or black skirts and blazers and we are colourful individuals who want to look sharp but feel too stuffy in our classic black, then step outside of that realm. My advice is to always be and look as professional as possible of course, but it doesn't have to be someone else's idea of professional. Be authentic to yourself, a pink shirt with a two-piece suit is perfectly acceptable. Or you are a woman that wants to add a splash of colour into her outfit, go for it and just keep it professional.

People who bring their authentic selves in all respects to work are not only more contented, they're much more productive. And it's easy to see why. People really shine when they are being their most authentic selves.

Particularly, in the workplace, depending on the situation we are in, we will adopt these masked personas because for some reason or another, we think it's easier to be another person than being ourselves. We hide behind this almost alter ego, to help us cope. We are in fact, all guilty of this currently or have been at some point in our lives. Doing this to get by in life can be hazardous to our health, certainly to our sense of self, we leave our workplace and can get angry that we allowed ourselves to be that person again. And the more entrenched we get in that behaviour, the more some of us believe what we are saying, yet always know that it isn't our best self and we become internally conflicted.

In this industry you will come across many agents who wear the mask, many quoting themselves as being #1 as an example. I wrote an article in a local magazine about WHAT ACHIEVING #1 MEANS, due to the frustration I felt about this statement.

"Real Estate agents often portray themselves as being # 1 in their respective field. If every agent appears to be number one, what value does the title hold? How do Buyers and Sellers differentiate between which number one holds the true value? With all the claims of the esteemed #1 title around, how can it be confirmed? Being number one in any field is no easy feat. It takes endless work, dedication, and true pride. That is why it is important to understand what being at the top in Real Estate means.

Being #1 entails having the best service possible as a realtor while being continuously successful with client transactions. Having supporting evidence is crucial when claiming to be the best of the best. For the past three years, I have achieved the status of being #1 Real Estate Agent in my area. Now, what makes me the true number one in all of my area? I have with hard work, honesty, and professionalism, achieved this status.

Being number one is a proud title to own. Excelling amongst competition is very satisfying as an agent, proving that the service I guarantee is one that is trusted very deeply. I happily offer the resources and the sacrifice that a true number one should offer.

When deciding on an agent, I encourage Buyers and Sellers to ask the agent specific questions about their services to see if they're the right fit. When they say that they are number one, ask the questions, "where do you stand as a number one?" and "what does your title as number one signify?". Some may attempt to alter the perspective of what being #1 means, which can be unfair to the public, and discredit those who sacrifice monumental amounts of time to earn their spot. Offering a great realtor experience is extremely important to us, and our efforts as strong realtors verify why we are #1.

Being a Real Estate agent is hard work. Being number one does not always mean that they are the best, but it demonstrates the countless times they've been trusted and successful in their tasks. Any successful agent deserves proper gratification and congratulations. While being number one in an office or a team is difficult, accomplishing the feat of being number one in all of my local area demonstrates how I go the extra mile with endless effort and large amounts of pride.

It is important to know which #1 stands above all the others, and in my area, I am the true number one in Real Estate based on volume and sales. I outsell my nearest competition by over 30%! I know where I stand.

I outsell all teams and all individuals (in my area). I have more listings than all teams/individuals, highest volume sales, and outsell the average agent by 25 to 1."

Some agents may tell you they are #1. He might be #1 in the office, but there's only him and his broker in that office! He adds an Asterix after stating he's the #1 agent in the area (but in the disclaimer it's based on one street north and south of him). A different picture was painted than reality. Is he lying? Not really. It may be ridiculous and bordering on unethical, but it's not totally illegal. When choosing the right agent, ask where they stand!

Research has shown that wearing a mask in the work environment can hinder the relationship building process, as those around us can detect signs of inconsistency in our behaviours, hence leading them to mistrust us. In addition, it can be tremendously stressful, continually swapping out masks.

However, there is a fine and unspoken line that we should be hesitant to cross with being perfectly authentic. I don't want to get anyone in trouble here. There are those who argue that we should be wary of being our fully authentic selves in the working environment, and that honest sharing of thoughts, feelings, and experiences at work can be risky. Despite its potential benefits, it can fail if it's hastily perceived or spoken at the wrong time, or to the wrong person; or if it is inconsistent with cultural norms of your office. This could end up negatively affecting your reputation, alienating clients or colleagues, nurturing a doubt, and ultimately deterring teamwork. Knowing when it's appropriate to talk about or reveal certain things shouldn't mean we can't be ourselves. I have seen great benefits in my own life with colleagues and clients.

"If you are a piano, don't try to be a violin. Be the true instrument that you are because it produces a beautiful and unique sound that is well needed within your organization." — Mike MacIsaac

As humans, it's our first instinct to show up authentically and to be our true selves. Authenticity is the daily practice of letting go of who we think we're supposed to be and embracing who we are.

However, somewhere between kindergarten and high school, we learn to start covering up our true selves and angling our persona towards being who we think others want us to be. This is typically the fitting in that we do throughout life, as a child, and right through to old age, in some way or another. Once we have satisfied our health and safety needs, we then look to fulfill the third level, our need for love and belonging. Our desire to fit in and belong becomes more important than the esteem and self-actualization needs that come after.

The need for social acceptance and fitting in all slowly chips away at our authenticity. We layer ourselves with facades in the desire for acceptance. These are the things that create emotional and intellectual barriers, preventing our colleagues, bosses, family and friends from seeing our true, authentic selves. And over time we don't know what that true authentic self looks like. It can be a difficult journey, if you allow the inauthenticity to get too deep where you lose yourself. My recommendation is that you don't let that happen, start to get a grip of your real being as soon as you read this.

When we show up without pretense, we connect easily, our life has more meaning, and we are easily more successful and consequentially much less stressed. And, like most things, if we want to get good at being our truer selves, we need to persevere and repeat the behaviour until it becomes second nature. Progress is noticing when we don't show up, true to ourselves, and using the awareness to correct our behavior and words. In doing so, we feel less fraught, we are more harmonious, and people look to us for direction.

What will happen over time as you start to get a better understanding of yourself with all its powerful revelations, you will start to feel better about who you really are. You will get excited as you start to notice a metamorphosis occur in the following ways:

- ☐ ***Accept yourself.*** This becomes glaringly tangible. A real clarity will begin to arise within yourself. You will slowly start to see some behaviours that no longer reflect who you are and no longer serve you. At first, it's difficult and takes a real mindfulness to undo these entrenched traits but it becomes easier as time goes on.

- ☐ You will find people are starting to gravitate to you more; and as a result, your client base starts to increase because they find it easy to be around you. Your thoughts, decisions and actions start to reflect who you are, not who you think you should be. Conformity starts to take a back seat to authenticity. This doesn't happen overnight, but it does happen, trust me.

- **Transformation:** This sets in to become the new norm. You may start to see character flaws that you weren't aware of during your veiled inauthentic journey. They can be scary and unsettling, but don't despair, this process is healthy. As you grow in your authenticity, you will find it easier to have uncomfortable conversations. We all have an innate desire to be liked. However, to get action and results, you must get contented with this discomfort. It's often in these moments that you not only help others gain clarity, but *you* have a professional growth moment, too. The instinctual feeling, we have when we step out of our comfort zone is simply not knowing how this will turn out. Embrace the old you as this helps set the stage for the new you. It's about getting a clear understanding of what you may have holding you back from success in real estate and personally. You will instinctively become more honest, with yourself and consequently with others. This will ultimately be projected outward to the world that you live in and others will really start to react differently with you.

- **Boundaries** in all aspects of your life become more relevant. You may have been a doer overtime, taking on others' responsibilities because you thought it was helping you fit in. A mindfulness comes into play where you are not completely self-serving, but you really want to do all you can to be a successful real estate professional. So, you'll ask more of yourself as to how you get there rather than, how do I fit in. It's a liberating metamorphosis. The more you know yourself, the more you see where you end, and another begins in life.

- **People of substance** will soon become who show up in your life. Like attracts like. As you think, so you are. These people will fill you with energy, they have good characters and they live with integrity. They take responsibility for their mistakes and subsequently apologize without reservation.

These are the same people if they have an uncomfortable conversation, they need to have with you, they come to you directly. Because of this, you'll attract better deals, you will make clearer decisions, and your motives will be purer, so you will make less mistakes. Again, people will gravitate to your authentic self because there is a positive energy that you will by osmosis, naturally emit. Your honesty in business will shine through, but more importantly, your honesty about who you are and what you want to achieve in your life will shine as well.

It takes less time and energy to show up as your true self. *Authenticity* is the gift that keeps on giving. As you show up without pretense, others start practicing it too, leading to a life with more solid people in it than not.

"Authenticity is more than speaking; Authenticity is also about doing. Every decision we make says something about who we are" —Simon Sinek

CHAPTER 14

Be The Best You Can Be

We have all been gifted with a certain skillset, be it positive or negative. But also, let's acknowledge that we also all have shortcomings.

"We are great at some things, but not good at everything."

Everyone is unique in their DNA and their skillsets vary. They could be for example, Athletic, Funny, Good Talkers, Great Mathematicians, Visionary, Calm, Great Negotiators, etc.

I have learned to maximize my skills and become an expert in the area of my strength's skills. With my weakness, I choose to improve in these areas by reaching out for help and/or recruiting people that could strengthen my weaker skillset to expand my organization. There are many profiling techniques and products out on the market (Example Disc Profiler and Colour profiler) that try and showcase your skills and promise to improve your weaknesses; as we are aware, these products are not cheap. Everyone becomes an expert in trying to improve you. You should be knowledgeable about what people enjoy about you and strengthen that.

I wasn't brought up with technical expertise and grew up in a more unstructured environment. I feel this has allowed me to use my people-skills to better understand the environment I am working in. My parents grew up in a rural town in southern Italy before immigrating to Canada. Both had very strong work ethics, which they passed on to my siblings and I. We were not pushed academically, rather raised with an old school belief of simply working hard. I believe this actually strengthened my understanding of the basic and fundamentals of how to relate to people in life and business.

I meet many people in our trade who have multiple degrees, with letters after their names, yet they many times are not the highest producers. In fact, some are terrible realtors. A dear friend of mine once said to me that "the difference between educated and uneducated people is, the educated person has been taught and programmed to analyze before he takes the next step, whereas the uneducated person would tend to jump right into a situation using a gut feeling to maneuver through opportunities.

Both mindsets have their advantages but knowing when to read opportunities can give you an edge above the competition.

There are many examples of Rags to Riches stories of how people who learned from the school of hard knocks, were able to use their mindset to create unbelievable success:

Russian business tycoon and Chelsea Football Club owner Roman Abramovich was born into poverty and orphaned at age 2.

Starbucks's Howard Schultz grew up in a housing complex for the poor.

Born into poverty, and suffered sexual abuse, Oprah Winfrey became the first African American TV correspondent in Tennessee.

Celine Dion was born to a large, poverty-stricken French-Canadian family (the youngest of 14 children). She now has over $400million to her name.

Justin Bieber

Not so long ago, before Justin Bieber became a YouTube sensation. The young Canadian was destitute, living in a rat-infested house with hardly any food. The young pop prince didn't even have his own bedroom and had to sleep on a pull-out couch. Today, he's worth over $65million.

These 'Rags to Riches' examples have shown me that many times, humble upbringing does not necessarily equal hardships later in life, rather it can be a catalyst to a successful life and career. Adversity can create a resilient and tough mindset necessary in business. These inspirational examples show us that no matter how bleak our future may look, you cannot only overcome hardship, but also thrive as a result of it. There is always an opportunity to excel!

What made these people successful is their self-awareness and recognition of their gifts and talents and even through both their financial and personal obstacles, they were able to overcome their shortcomings to reach monumental success. There have been times, I have felt envious of how some people grew up (with all the opportunities that helped them become polished and educated within a wealthy environment), but I have seen that a structured upbringing can at times be somewhat limiting, not allowing a sense of wonder to wander off their pre-determined course and create their own future founded on a fire in the belly, to succeed in what someone is born to do or is passionate about!

My humble beginnings were very happy, even though we had many financial challenges. We always had food on the table, but lacked the comfortable extras such as toys, family trips, etc. We had no family vehicle and my parents never spoke a word of English. They surrounded themselves with fellow Italians.

My parents had instilled in me very strong work ethics. I had seen the struggles they endured that I knew I did not want for myself. As I grew older, I did not want my family and I, wife and children to face these similar hardships and was certain to use my motivated personality to achieve success.

I was always a driven personality. When I put my mind to something, I wanted to excel in it. My first job as a youngster was delivering newspapers. I would get up at 5am and finish my run by 8:30. Each day, I challenged myself to finish earlier than the last, until I shaved almost an hour off my time.

When I ran, I ran to be first! When I played sports, I excelled to make the school teams. I took up squash and quickly reached top of my game at club level. I saw my drive to win as a gift.

Being of 1 of 8 siblings, we all had different personalities, unique gifts and differing skill sets. As an adolescent, school was not my favorite environment; in fact, I feared it. I was always happier in a social setting amongst my close friends. I enjoyed parties, sports and socializing. I was quite the partier! It was well known that Tav Schembri would always be on the invite list to any party!

Looking back, the socializing in school gave me great confidence and an ability to engage in networking with a variety of different personalities. I had no fear of large groups, organizing events and mingling with people from different walks of life. This was an example where instead of textbook learning, I became more street savvy through my ability to converse with people from all walks of life. This had taught me that regardless of a person's wealth or education, I could always find common ground. And as I reached adulthood, I wasn't intimidated talking to wealthy or poor, blue collar or white collar, it simply didn't matter, we always had something to talk about, making an instant connection!

As I entered the Real Estate industry, I applied the same approach. Carefully watching the top producers in our industry and pushing myself to achieve the best, I made a promise to myself to put 2 solid years of hard work and 100% commitment using my skillsets to a maximum. I trained my mind to think outside the box and excelled like the top producers!

The training the industry coaches were providing (their approach being more cautious) was heavily based on following the rule, similar to an educational system, for which I had a fear of from my school days.

I started looking closely at the training material of industry experts and training coaches, soon realizing that (although correct) in my mind I thought they were impractical and unrealistic. The training costs involved were not affordable for start-up realtors. The costs involved can run into tens of thousands of dollars and their teaching process was slow. They were demanding long-term commitments that took precious time away from actually selling grassroots real estate and the practical side of the industry.

This book breaks away from the traditional industry format. It allows you to gain insight and learn from my experience. I feel it will snowball the process to involve yourself in the true real estate industry, which for me is Buying and Selling. After spending a few hours reading this book, you should be comfortable in zoning in on your skillsets and confidently discuss buying and selling in real estate.

My advice through this chapter is to *show up* — every time, every day and in most every situation! Stop avoiding challenges; you should have the mindset to face all challenges head on with dedication. If you do not deal with them *now*, they will not just disappear; they will confront you tomorrow. You will find that dealing with these real-life issues will make you a stronger and more successful person as a Realtor.

You must realise that every human deals with issues on a daily basis and how you confront yours will ultimately dictate the outcome. Using common sense with how you view hardships, you will learn to see that they are not only unique to you; it's part of life, you may as well get over it!

Remember, whether you lose a deal, experience a financial hardship, or even deal with serious health issues, whatever situation sends you from high to low (even if you think you'll never make it through the challenge) you always do! Take a minute to look back over your life right now and remember a time when everything looked dark and bleak, yet here you are here, months and years later, still going strong! You are living proof that you'll make it through anything you put your mind to.

I have faced some traumatic situations in my life, one being a woodworking accident that completely changed the trajectory of my life. I believe my strong and positive attitude helped me overcome the odds and catapulted me to the upper tier of the Real Estate industry.

Anyone who has ever trained for competitive sports knows the importance of the opposition. No matter who or what appears as an obstacle on their path, they know to win they must focus on remaining positive. They may stumble, but they will always get up and show up for the next practice, the next experience or in your case, the next deal. In real estate, that can be the winning recipe for success: learn to get up when you fall because you will fall, but the key is to always get back up! This is how it is in life in general! Be your optimum self and be set for all the good that lies ahead. Show the world that you mean business and you are only going to move forward, period. When you show up, the world knows you're serious about playing and believing that you will become a victor. That is exactly how you must face each day, make the calls, have the right attitude, look your best and show up!

The same is true for all of us as we move along our journey in real estate. There will be many times when we feel discouraged, perhaps even to the point of wanting to give up, but if we decide we want to make a dream come true, we must continue to focus on that desire and keep it in our minds every day, all day long, especially when we feel defeated.

The secret to making it, in creating your dream is to believe in the success that belongs to you and let go of the need to make excuses for not showing up. When excuses happen, like you can't make it to a meeting because you didn't do the homework for the client or some similar, let it go and just show up anyway!

Imagine what you want from your career and keep it at the top of your mind constantly. Accordingly, visualize this; see yourself sitting in your brand-new Audi r8 Coupe and showing up at a client's home in your awesome new wheels. Or envision yourself in the grand home you've always dreamed of with your children in great academic schools. Visualize all the advantages that you ever wanted for them, materializing. Visualizing engraves dreams and goals into your mind's eye. You can do the same. Picture the result of what you want, always keep it in your mind. Dress up for the win as if you have already become the winner. What will happen? When the timing is right, the vision of what you wanted will manifest in your life, just like you saw it or maybe, even better. You'll close that deal, make a lot of money or whatever you had planned for yourself before it even manifested.

There will be periods in your life that will show you exactly the reverse of what you wanted or what you had planned. You'll look around you and maybe think it's all a lie. The world can be funny that way. The first few hours of the work day can have a significant effect on your level of productivity over the following hours, so it's important you have a morning routine that allows your best foot forward and ultimately more focus and greater chance for daily success.

Here are some great ways to start your day, give some of them or all of them a try:

Don't be late: This may be logical to most people, but some don't realize that showing up late will not only leave a negative impression and make someone feel that you are disrespecting their time, and that they are not important but it can also throw off your entire day. Getting in on time or better yet, a little early helps your mindset for the day and helps promote a feeling of accomplishment.

Begin fresh each day: You may have to attend to all sorts of things where real estate is concerned or continue discussions that are residuals from the day before, that's common. But try to leave yesterday where it is and begin fresh with a new day attitude. Many people feel that their wits are best in the morning, and that is when they are most creative and productive.

Be consistently cheerful: Pay close attention to your mood as it can have a negative impact on people around you. A positive attitude when you arrive at the office, is congruent to who you are as a person, let it be your trademark. Cheery and positive will always get the win.

Be organized: The first hour of the work day is the best time to prioritize and focus on what you unquestionably need to complete, especially in real estate. Too many people get distracted first thing in the morning with minor details, when there may be considerably more important issues that need attending to. My best advice here is to keep good lists of to-dos and update them regularly. It's best to update at the end of the day or first thing in the morning, keep it updated as the day progresses.

Don't be pretentious — no one is that important: Taking time to connect with people you work with is essential, and doing small things like eye contact, smiling, asking them about their evening and checking in on what they may need help with, helps you as a leader or a colleague, keeps a pulse, and helps set the tone for your colleagues. And seriously, it takes less than 5 minutes to make people feel valued, and it helps everyone understand the collective goals. And by sharing your goals for the day publicly, considerably increases the chances of execution.

Keep a tidy work environment: A neat work environment sets a message for the day. An upset work area leads to a cluttered mind. If you have set up reminders for yourself and they don't stand out, how do you expect to see it? A clutter-free workspace leads to a clutter-free mind. In a perfect world, cleaning your desk would happen nightly or first thing in the morning. Best chance for focus and productivity is a clean desk.

Get to important communications first thing in the morning. If you are going to make an important call or send e-mails, do this first thing in the morning wherever possible. It will help you get a solid direction for your day. You may have to go meet a client at their property, it's better to arrange that after an early morning email or call. If you have your questions ready and your e-mails are sent off as soon as possible in the morning, by the end of the day, you should have what you need to set up for the next day and on.

I want to give you some things to consider in business and in your personal life. It's basically as follows, how you show up for life is how your life turns out.

I've never been a fan of people pulling the victim card because the fact of the matter is that when you look at life in reverse, you can see that the choices you've made have brought you to where you are right now. Consider the following way of looking at life when it comes to showing up and being the best, you can be at any given moment.

When your thoughts and intentions match your behavior, you are consistent, and you will look and feel like a person with honour. But if you say or think one thing, then do another, that's inconsistent. We are all apt to change our minds, regardless of the reason. It's human.

The key here is to be authentic and true to yourself, first and foremost. When you make commitments to yourself such as, losing weight and you go full power for a week or maybe two and then it just tapers off and ends up falling between the proverbial bed and wall, the result is that you have lost some underlying trust in yourself. And if this becomes a pattern, you are eating healthy for example, you do this for a period and don't keep it up, again, you're just being inconsistent with yourself. We tell ourselves we'll get to it, but then we don't. Something gets in the way and distracts us from our pledge. If you do things like that often, your subconscious mind doesn't trust you anymore. And since all our behavior stems from our subconscious mind, you end up creating events in your life that you don't want.

What may end up happening is situations like, you have trust issues, your health fails, your relationships suffer, etc. All this stuff happens because your subconscious mind doesn't believe what you say. It might sound weird, but your subconscious mind trusts what you tell it, so it will do what you tell it to do.

We all have those people in our lives that say that they are going to do something, but we really know that they won't do what they said they were going to do, it's really a bad handle to have. They will not typically do very well in life, maybe not terribly, but they are essentially not very trustworthy and certainly not people who you can depend on in life.

If you say you're going to do something, and you do something else, and repeat that behavior repeatedly, then you are creating your own destiny, and people will see that in you. They may say that you don't walk your talk. Even though you know you do, they'll see the pattern you've been following in your own life and decide that you aren't someone that can be relied upon, sadly.

It all depends on how you want to *show up* — not just for other people, but more importantly for yourself. You can even be trustworthy and dependable to others, but if you're not that to yourself, you will find life a lot harder than it should be.

Showing up as who you are on the inside, is honesty. And when you are consistent, you are being the best person you can possibly be, even if you think you could be better. You can say things like, I can do better, and if that motivates you, then it's terrific. But being the best is about showing up as yourself to begin with in all areas of your life.

This increased the trust I had in myself, and I started to be more compatible both in my inner world and my outer world. And of course, I was starting to trust my intuition again.

Consequently, no matter what is going on around you right now, don't remain in the predisposed position. Stand up and lift your head, so you can see all the possibilities. Dress yourself with the power and drive that you must create your dreams into reality. When you have a belief, the world just aligns with you and begins the process of bringing everything into completion. As you show up, the universe shows up, and solutions to every problematic situation occurs, allowing your ideas to manifest, all in divine timing. It's not always easy to see the good when things feel like they are falling apart, but in the end, as you look back over the resolve of the situation, the good will appear. It's your choice of course, but I can promise that it always pays off to Get up! Dress up! and most importantly Show up!

"What would life be if we had no courage to attempt anything?"—Vincent van Gogh

Here are some things to keep in mind, because this is what your client is thinking about when deciding on a real estate agent.

Will they communicate with me? As a house seller or buyer, it can be stressful dealing with an agent who is not great at communication. The real estate market is time sensitive, so you need an agent who will let you know quickly where you stand with your current buying or selling situation, so you can move on quickly to another property or potential buyer. It's of the utmost importance that agents stay in close contact with their clients and customers. What seems like insignificant information to an agent who has been in the business for years can be important to clients who are new to the real estate climate. Rapid and clear responses are a must in a real estate agent.

Look at it this way, your clients keep calling you, but you're not giving them enough information. The key element of being proactive is keeping the client well informed.

- A good agent will always have their client's needs as their top priority. Buying and selling houses can be stressful and it's important for the agent to make sure that the client is feeling supported and happy. A good agent knows their client's success is their success.

On the flip side, good communication also means mastering the art of listening. Listening and knowing when to talk and when not to talk, may just be one of the most important skills to learn in business negotiations. It is all too easy to talk yourself out of a deal, as I had learned early on in my career. Learning to understand whilst talking less could not only get you a client, but it could save you one too!

Here are a some of my personal experiences that taught me a valuable lesson about listening more and talking less:

The most important time to be mindful of what you say, may just be right when you're about to sign off on the deal, as I learned a few years back working with a colleague of mine. I was in a situation where I had a difficult time trying to get the owners to agree on a price. One of the clients was adamant the house was worth more. He nostalgically reminisced about how much work his Father had put into the house, how he built the garage with his own hands out of solid concrete and what the home meant to him and his family. We finally had him agreeing to the offer, when my colleague started acknowledging all the hard work his Father had done, stating how much he appreciated the craftsmanship, emphasizing the sweat, money and hard work he could see was put into the home.

Unknowingly to my colleague, what seemed like praise and innocent banter, had inadvertently pushed our client into backing off completely.

The client suddenly changed his mind, saying the home had "too much sentimental value". He refused to sign the offer and just like that, the deal fell through!

Another example of 'talking yourself out of a deal' happened early on in my real estate career. I was showing a house in the suburbs to a couple that seemed very interested in the property. The husband asked my colleague and I, if there were schools near by, instead of keeping it simple and stating there were 2 great schools in the area, we assumed close proximity of schools was going to be a great selling feature that would help get us an offer. So, with excitement, we talked up just how close these schools were, how they were within easy walking distance, then continuing on into even further detail, how one school was just up the street and the other was only a couple streets away! Little did we know; the buyers didn't see this as a positive at all; in fact, they saw it as a deal breaker! The husband quickly lost interest all together, saying "we aren't interested in living in an area where there are ton of noisy, children passing by the house twice a day!"

And lastly, being a good listener can create trust and confidence. It is a helpful skill in both personal and business relationships. There's an old saying that the squeaky wheel gets the oil. It's important to look at all feedback, the good and the bad. Listening to your client empowers them. At the end of the day, people want to feel heard; even the clients that seem most difficult to work with, simply want to feel like their thoughts and ideas mattered. The negative clients could also be the ones that help you streamline your business. By finding the gaps that may need filling, managing complaints and problems, etc. take the good feedback and share it. Positive feedback should be shared on websites, brochures, and more. It can be some of your best marketing! And use the bad feedback to learn and improve your skills and business.

Keep in mind that it's your client(s) that will be the deciding factor in your real estate success. A good rule of thumb is to think about how you would like to be treated and treat your client the same way.

Real estate transactions are probably the biggest deal that will happen in a person's life and if you are professionally dressed, knowledgeable and authentic, you have just surpassed much of your competition. Good luck and go out there to make a difference in peoples' lives as well as in your own life!

CHAPTER 15

Final Word of Guidance

When I started in this industry, I developed an immediate passion for the whole experience, literally from start to finish. I decided early on that I had one kick at the can to get this right from the start. And I'm not kidding when I say I have used <u>all</u> the advice that I have given throughout this book and I continue to use it. My daily practices are set in stone, from personal presentation to living authentically and everything in-between. When you don't have to sweat the small stuff, you will find your day unfolds as it should, professionally and productively.

Throughout my career in Real Estate, I have come across just about every personality type you could imagine and just about every scenario of hurdles and successes you could think. I started with humble beginnings and organically evolved into a successful businessman, both in the Business industry and Real Estate through much hard work. And the pieces of advice in this book are what have worked for me and I do integrate these practices into my life, both personally and professionally, so I can tell you firsthand, these are effective tools to jumpstart your life as a MILION DOLLAR AGENT.

Because I have been a long-time businessman, I can clearly see the things that had been barriers to my success over the years and the keys to my success. These barriers and subsequent successes have given me the wisdom that has ultimately meant so much for me that I wanted to share this with you.

I struggled like any other individual in business, but I took very good notes along the way on what I needed to do to evolve the way I have been able to over the years. I'm not sure that if I had not had "the accident," I would have ended up in real estate. I look at that accident quite fondly now, because I'm literally living my dream with a great career and financial freedom.

I feel very fortunate that I chose to go in a different direction in my career and I'm particularly pleased that it was in this industry. It's truly hard to imagine my life any other way than the way it is right now. I can literally be at the office in five minutes, I employ several members of my family and as an added bonus, I'm a Million Dollar Agent.

My success and my failures are completely my own. My three children bring me great joy and they are all successful in their own rights. I couldn't be prouder to be their father. And it's all because I have worked hard, and ultimately, I own my own business. I have the indulgences that are afforded to someone that has achieved a level of financial freedom.

We have many great parties at our home that include people like clients, prospective clients, politicians, family and friends. Being able to do these things, to me, are marks of success and are all an important part of my life and some of the many things I am grateful for. We drive very nice vehicles and can afford most anything we want. Financial freedom is something most people try to achieve, and I feel I have reached this goal for my needs — with all that in 5 short years in this business.

As I mentioned earlier in this book, the entire trajectory of my life changed because of a single moment in time. We don't always know what life holds for us and sometimes we must listen to our gut and take chances. I believe this wholeheartedly.

My hope is that if you're reading this chapter, which is my conclusion, then you've read the book and you've found the information straightforward, logical and most importantly, applicable. I hope that you also take this information and become the success you are meant to be. Because if you didn't want to be successful, you wouldn't have picked up this book to begin with!

The suggestions I've written about will definitely set you on your path for making a real success of yourself and will also set you on your way to becoming a *Million Dollar Agent.*

I have outlined all the aspects involved for you to make a real difference in your life. Once you get these steps in place, you will have all the groundwork necessary to bring yourself to the next level in a successful future in real estate.

Finally, here are some of my top tips I'd like to leave you with:

10 Ways to Start and Stay Strong in Real Estate

1. Work with the Best

When I decided to get into real estate, I wanted to deal with the best in the industry. I now know I'm working with the best in the world – and that feels good. I think the

RE/MAX brand has helped me tremendously, especially starting out. Belonging to RE/MAX helped me establish a strong reputation, no question about it.

2. Love What You Do

When you choose a career that you really enjoy, it doesn't even feel like work. I have no problem getting up in the morning, getting a jump on my work and working as late as I can — every day. I know at some point I'll have to slow down, but right now, it's quite easy for me.

3. Nurture Relationships

As a hairstylist, I was really well-known in the area. I kept in contact with my past clients, and we had some get-togethers. One thing led to another and clients after former clients ended up listing properties and buying with me. Once it started, it just kept going. Contacts from the past and referrals from my hairstyling clients helped me get started.

4. Understand Your Clients

My strength is being able to read what people are really saying, even if they're saying something else. When we go to negotiate, a lot of times I just put the facts on the table and let the clients do most of the negotiating. That way, it's not a hard sell at all. They're very comfortable with it because I've done all my homework for them and they have all the information.

5. Lead with Confidence

Every Associate has to learn how to have or build up their confidence. Real estate is a tough industry, so you need to feel confident. A lot of strategy and discipline is required to succeed, and being rejected once, twice, three times is just going to help you strategize how to reach the ultimate goal: selling or buying a property. Always go into listing presentations thinking you're going to get the listing.

6. **Compete to Succeed**

Whenever I get into something — it doesn't matter what it is — I always strive to be the best. I don't just test the waters. If I'm going to get into it, then I'm going to do the best I can Headfirst. And that's what I've done in real estate. If you need coaching or help, get it. Realize your shortcomings and make them stronger. Don't try to reinvent the wheel. In the meantime, use your strengths to your advantage.

7. **Speak the Truth**

During my first listing presentation, the homeowners asked me how many homes I had sold in the past. It's the question all new agents dread. And I just said to them, 'I've got to be honest. You're my first customers, but I will work extra hard to sell your place. I know I can do the job; I'm confident about it.' There was some hesitation; the husband and wife looked at each other, and then they signed the contract. If you're honest, someone will give you the opportunity.

8. **Overcome Your Fears**

Builders intimidate a lot of new agents because they have a lot of money and knowledge. But I find that one of the big pluses of real estate is bringing two parties together. I get a lot of builders approaching me now, which I never thought would happen. They see my signs; they know me now and they call me on a regular basis.

9. **Give Back to The Industry**

I networked with the top agents at Remax during an Elite Retreat and this allowed me the secrets of their success. Seeing videos and listening carefully, they had many things in common. They were true professionals. It gives me great pleasure to create my own someday to share my secrets with new agents and experienced ones to help them boost their sales.

10. **First Impressions Do Work**

Not only your attire should be professional, your hair (and makeup) should be also. A Well Pressed Suit and Foil Accent Highlights with a Metrosexual Current Clean Cut go a long way to Success. If your hair is not looking great, there is a good chance you will not get the deal. Your clients will say, if they are not looking after themselves, how can they look after me?

I'll leave you with this final thought…

"The secret to getting ahead in life is to focus your energy not on yesterday, but on building and growing something new right now."

TESTIMONIALS

"As a career realtor, I have had the pleasure of meeting and working with some of the best in the business, but Tav Schembri takes best to new heights; constant, professional and perfectionist, always classy. And most importantly, he puts his family and clients first."

Adam Schickedanz

Broker, Re/Max All-Stars Realty

Top 10 network wide 2016, 2017 and 2018